Old-Time Advertising Cuts and Typography

184 Plates from
the Boston Type and Stereotype Foundry Catalog (1832)

Edited by
STEPHEN O. SAXE

Dover Publications, Inc.

New York

Published in Canada by General Publishing Company, Ltd.,
30 Lesmill Road, Don Mills, Toronto, Ontario.
Published in the United Kingdom by Constable and Company, Ltd.,
10 Orange Street, London WC2H 7EG.

This Dover edition, first published in 1989, is a republication (slightly abridged, as described in the introduction) of *Specimen of Printing Types from the Boston Type & Stereotype Foundry,* as originally published in Boston in 1832. A new introduction has been written specially for the Dover edition by Stephen O. Saxe.

Mr. Saxe also furnished his copy of the original work for reproduction. American Type Founders Company Library, Rare Book and Manuscript Library, Columbia University, provided pp. 1–7, 19, 20, 24, 27, 35, 55, 99, 103, 116, 117, 122, 131, 163, 169 and 174–184 for reproduction. The Department of Printing and Graphic Arts, The Houghton Library, Harvard University, provided pp. 162 and 170 for reproduction. The editor and publisher would like to extend their thanks to both institutions for their cooperation.

DOVER *Pictorial Archive* SERIES

This book belongs to the Dover Pictorial Archive Series. You may use the designs and illustrations for graphics and crafts applications, free and without special permission, provided that you include no more than ten in the same publication or project. (For permission for additional use, please write to Dover Publications, Inc., 31 East 2nd Street, Mineola, N.Y. 11501.)

However, republication or reproduction of any illustration by any other graphic service whether it be in a book or in any other design resource is strictly prohibited.

Manufactured in the United States of America
Dover Publications, Inc., 31 East 2nd Street, Mineola, N.Y. 11501

Library of Congress Cataloging-in-Publication Data

Boston Type and Stereotype Foundry.
    [Specimen of printing types from the Boston Type & Stereotype Foundry]
    Old-time advertising cuts and typography : 184 plates from the Boston Type and Stereotype Foundry catalog (1832) / edited by Stephen O. Saxe.
        p.   cm. — (Dover pictorial archive series)
    Reprint, with new introd. Originally published: Specimen of printing types from the Boston Type & Stereotype Foundry. Boston : The Foundry, 1832.
    Bibliography: p.
    ISBN 0-486-26023-2
    1. Printing—Specimens. 2. Boston Type and Stereotype Foundry. 3. Type and type-founding—Massachusetts—Boston. 4. Printing—Massachusetts—Boston—History—19th century—Sources. 5. Advertising—Massachusetts—Boston—History—19th century—Sources. I. Saxe, Stephen O. II. Title. III. Series.
Z250.B737   1989   89-32191
                                                            CIP

Introduction

Over 150 years ago, the Boston Type and Stereotype Foundry issued this catalog of type and illustrations to printers. For most of the years following, the few surviving copies were of no interest to anyone. But time has at last brought the attention of typographers, graphic designers and others to the wealth of material presented in this specimen book.

Having begun business in 1817, the Boston Type Foundry was only 15 years old in 1832, when this specimen of its types and ornaments was issued. The foundry had been started as a branch of the New York foundry of Elihu White, one of the first in the United States. White also established a foundry in Cincinnati in 1817, the first west of the Allegheny Mountains. White sold his Cincinnati and Boston branches to local owners, the Boston foundry in 1819 to Timothy Bedlington, a bookbinder, and Charles Ewer, a bookseller.

Neither of these men had the skills needed to operate a type foundry. They hired a manager, Edward Haskell, who in turn hired skilled mechanics in the field of typefounding: Michael Dalton (later an owner of the rival Dickinson Type Foundry in Boston) and Edward Pelouze (later owner of his own New York foundry).

The foundry issued its first specimen book in 1820—a small pamphlet of 34 pages. Every year after that, new typefaces and ornaments were added to the foundry's offerings, so that by the time the 1832 specimen was issued, the book was over five times the length of the first specimen.

This expansion was the result of the sale of the foundry by Bedlington and Ewer to another bookseller, Timothy H. Carter, who brought in new capital, moved the foundry to a new building in Harvard Place and arranged to begin stereotyping, in addition to typecasting. The stereotype process created flat printing plates from pages of printing type. A plaster impression was made of a page of type or a wood engraving, and into this mold molten lead alloy was poured to create the stereotype plate. Thus, type was freed for other work. The name of the company was changed to the Boston Type and Stereotype Foundry, and James Conner, an experienced stereotyper, headed the department. A few years later, he used his savings to start one of the largest type foundries in New York.

In 1823, the foundry moved to a larger building on Salem Street, next to the Christ Church (otherwise known as the Old North Church, later made famous by Longfellow's "Paul Revere's Ride"). A fire on June 23 of the following year interrupted operations of the foundry. A move in 1829 took the foundry to 37 & 39 Congress Street, the address from which this specimen book was issued. Later locations included Spring Lane and 104 Milk Street.

Of the many buildings occupied by the Boston Type Foundry, not a brick or a scrap of timber is likely to have survived. The type it manufactured over its span of 75 years in business is almost as elusive—collectors of nineteenth-century printing type may have a total of 100 or so fonts of type with the Boston Type Foundry pinmark. Its most enduring legacy is a small group of fragile type specimens.

The foundry issued about 46 different specimen books, which today are in the collections of about 20 individuals and libraries. A grand total of about 120 copies of all editions have been located, although undoubtedly there are more in bookshops and attics and on the shelves of other individuals and institutions. In 12 years of seeking American type-foundry specimens, I have collected ten different specimens of the 46 the Boston Type Foundry issued between 1820 and 1889.

These specimens, while not "rare books," are nevertheless not commonly found. But their value today lies less in their scarcity than in their usefulness and in the interest they hold for today's reader.

Fashion often follows commerce, and commerce in early nineteenth-century America was changing. Small cities were becoming mercantile centers. The Industrial Revolution was changing the way things were made and done. Handwork was giving way to machine work; ingenious Yankees were dreaming up new ways to speed the manufacture of everything. Mills were built; canals and steamboats were opening up the interior of the country to commerce; business was growing. Typography reflected the new need to advertise goods and services. Type designs became larger, bolder and more attention-getting. All these changes are reflected in the type shown in this specimen book.

In 1832, display typefaces were a recent phenomenon. The first ones, called "fat faces," started to appear in England shortly after 1806. These faces are still in use today, and are known as "ultra Bodoni"—that is, Bodoni typefaces made very heavy. Their first use, both in England and in this country, was for lottery advertisements and posters. (See pages 16 to 32 for examples; related cuts showing cornucopias and other lottery symbols can be seen in cuts nos. 252, 365, 367 and 374–377.) The fat faces were soon followed by ornamented faces (pages 54 to 61), which became very popular. Of the types shown in the Boston

Type Foundry's first specimen in 1820, only about half a dozen could be called ornamented. They were essentially classical roman letterforms with a drop shadow or inline added; in the 1832 specimen, there is page after page of highly ornamented faces. The new fashion was decoration and embellishment; the discreet, classically correct forms of the eighteenth century were falling out of favor.

Chart 1, containing most of the styles of display type offered in the 1832 specimen book, shows that almost all of the designs had originated in England only about 15 years before. Robert Thorne, William Caslon IV and Vincent Figgins were leading English typefounders of the period. Their innovations quickly found their way to America.

The nomenclature of early nineteenth-century type included two descriptive phrases. The first, indicating *style*, we have seen in Chart 1 (i.e., "shaded," "ornamented," etc.). The second phrase described the *size* of the type. The sizes of type in the English-speaking world had been traditional since William Caxton introduced printing into England in the late fifteenth century. Chart 2 gives these traditional names, the approximate modern equivalent in point sizes (introduced in this country in 1883) and a brief comment about the origin of the names.

CHART 1

FAT FACE
Introduced by Thorne,
ca. 1806

SHADED
Figgins, 1815

ANTIQUE
Figgins, 1815

OUTLINE
(FLUTED)
Figgins, 1815

BLACK
Figgins, 1815

ORNAMENTED
Various typefounders,
from ca. 1815

ITALIAN
Caslon, 1821

Pearl   5 point

Nonpareil   6 point

Minion   7 point

Brevier   8 point   The size of type used to print breviaries for the Church.

Bourgeois   9 point   A French word, perhaps reflecting the use of French in England in Caxton's time. May be named for the French city of Bourges, or for its use in cheap books intended for the bourgeoisie.

Long Primer   10 point   Primer was the name of an ecclesiastical book, for which this size of type was used.

Small Pica   11 point

Pica   12 point   From the Latin word for the table showing the course of services of the Church, which was printed in this size.

English   14 point   This size of type was extensively used by English printers of law books and the acts of Parliament.

Two Line Brevier   16 point

Great Primer   18 point

Paragon   20 point

Double Small Pica   22 point

Double Pica   24 point

Double English   28 point

Four line Brevier   32 point

Double Great Primer   36 point

Canon   48 point   This size was used for the beginning paragraphs of the printed canons of the Church.

By using the term "Double" or "____ Lines Pica," every size of type, no matter how large, could be described without the need for additional names.

From about 1830 to 1838 the Boston Type and Stereotype Foundry encouraged a young New York typefounder, David Bruce, Jr., in his efforts to mechanize type-casting. He developed a revolutionary new machine, the Bruce pivotal type caster. The machine eventually proved successful, and from the Boston foundry the Bruce caster spread to every corner of the world. It made possible the casting of far greater amounts of type and of far more ornate type, which was very difficult to cast by hand. It is, however, doubtful whether any of the types in this specimen were cast by the Bruce type-casting machine.

The changing scene reflected in typographic styles can be seen even more graphically in the "cuts" sold in the ornament and illustration section of the book. In this section the current state of American daily life and technology is shown: everything from steamboats (cuts nos. 90–94, etc.) to canal barges (cut no. 388), Franklin stoves (cut no. 401) and printing presses (cuts nos. 487–489). America was entering the Age of Steam, as can be seen by the steamboat cuts; but it was too early for steam railroads, which had just begun to develop in the 1830s. (A horse-drawn railway can be seen in cut no. 447.)

These illustrations were sold to printers for use in books, newspapers, almanacs and school primers. Cast as stereotype plates and mounted on a block of wood, type-high, they were sold ready to be printed with type on a hand or cylinder press. It was a process that served well, although it could not reproduce the fine lines of the delicate woodblocks produced by such artists as Thomas Bewick of England. The result is a simplified, strong image that has immediate impact on the eye. These images are quite different from the printer's ornaments produced later in the nineteenth century, after the invention of the electrotype plate (ca. 1845) made possible the exact reproduction of fine lines. In this reprint many of these unhackneyed images are made available to graphic artists for the first time.

We know very little about the artists who produced them. It is known that Dr. Alexander Anderson, America's first wood engraver, made many of them for type foundries. In this book, cuts nos. 30 and 360 are signed by him, and cut 365 is signed "A" and is probably by him. Another signature, "Bowen," can be found on cuts nos. 33, 250 and 619; cuts 126 and 456 are signed "B" and are probably by the same artist. Bowen is probably Abel Bowen (1790–1850), a wood engraver who organized the Boston Bewick Company in 1834.

The Boston Type Foundry resumed its original name (dropping "and Stereotype") in 1851 and remained one of the leading type foundries in the country. In 1872 the owners established a branch in St. Louis named the Central Type Foundry. The success of the branch was so great that in 1888 it was able to purchase the parent company, which continued to operate as a separate division. But the great era of American foundries came to an end in 1892, when, after a period of cutthroat competition, 23 foundries joined together to form the American Type Founders Company. The Boston Type Foundry was one of these, and although the name appeared on a few specimens for a year or two, after 1892 it was no longer an independent foundry.

The 1832 type specimen book reproduced here is a facsimile, all type and most cuts being in their original size. Almost every page of the original has the words BOSTON TYPE AND STEREOTYPE FOUNDRY following the specimen of type; they have been omitted to avoid unnecessary repetition. Folios have been added for this edition, but they do not necessarily match the exact pagination of the original. A few pages have been omitted from this reprint, including several pages of the smaller text types, and a few pages of geometric diagrams at the end (of which a sample page is reproduced). The original was printed on unwatermarked, dampened paper on one side of the sheet only, without pagination. The printer was Samuel N. Dickinson, a leading Boston printer who started his own type foundry in 1839. Because my copy, from which this facsimile was reproduced, lacked some pages, these were photographed from the copy in the American Type Founders Company Library at Columbia University. Two pages missing from both the Columbia copy and my own were reproduced from the copy at Harvard's Houghton Library. Grateful thanks are given to Rudolf Ellenbogen of Butler Library, Columbia, and to Eleanor M. Garvey of the Houghton Library, Harvard, for their assistance in reproducing these pages. Only three other copies are known: a copy sold by Dawson's Book Shop, Los Angeles, in 1979; one at the University of Virginia, Charlottesville; and one at the Newberry Library, Chicago.

Stephen O. Saxe

BIBLIOGRAPHY

Annenberg, Maurice. *Type Foundries of America and their Catalogs.* Baltimore: Maran Printing Services, 1975.

Gray, Nicolete. *Nineteenth-Century Ornamented Typefaces.* Second edition. Berkeley and Los Angeles: University of California Press, 1976.

Johnson, A. F. *Type Designs.* Third edition. London: André Deutsch, 1966.

Silver, Rollo. *Typefounding in America, 1787–1825.* Charlottesville: University Press of Virginia, 1965.

Wolpe, Berthold, ed. *Vincent Figgins Type Specimens, 1801 and 1815.* London: Printing Historical Society, 1967.

SPECIMEN

OF

PRINTING TYPES

FROM THE

Boston Type & Stereotype Foundry,

Nos. 37 & 39 CONGRESS STREET.

JOHN G. ROGERS, Agent.

BOSTON:

SAMUEL N. DICKINSON, PRINTER

1832.

ADVERTISEMENT.

—◦◦◦—

THE PRINTERS of the United States are respectfully invited to examine the Specimens from this Foundry, and may be assured that no pains are spared in producing Types, and other articles, of the best manufacture. The Company having been incorporated, are enabled to keep a large capital invested; and, of course, to supply extensive orders without the usual delay.

Printers (particularly of newspapers) are reminded, that founts of type, which have been used in Stereotyping, and but little worn, are kept generally on hand, and are offered at from fifteen to twenty-five per cent. discount.

STEREOTYPING executed on the most liberal terms, as to price and payment. Booksellers, and others, are referred to the late works stereotyped at the above Foundry.

Orders left at the Foundry, 39 Congress street, or addressed by mail to the subscriber, will be promptly attended to.

JOHN G. ROGERS, AGENT

Boston Type and Stereotype Foundry

Different faces cast to larger or smaller bodies.

N. B. This Book contains *no* specimens excepting of type cast at the above Foundry.

2

PRICES OF TYPE

AT THE

Boston Type and Stereotype Foundry.

SIX MONTHS, OR SIX PER CENT. DISCOUNT FOR CASH.

Roman and Italic, Plain.

Six line Pica, and all larger	$0	30
Five line Pica	0	30
Canon	0	30
Double Paragon	0	32
Double Great Primer	0	32
Double English	0	34
Double Pica	0	34
Great Primer	0	36
English	0	36
Pica	0	38
Small Pica	0	40
Long Primer	0	42
Bourgeois	0	46
Brevier	0	56
Minion	0	70
Nonpareil	0	90
Pearl	1	40
Two line Minion, and all larger two line letter	0	44
Two line Nonpareil	0	48
Two line Pearl	0	64

Bold Face.

Small Pica Capitals	0	64
L. Primer Cap's and Lower Case	0	64
Brevier Capitals	0	80
Minion Capitals and Lower Case	1	00

Blacks.

Five line Pica	0	50
Five line Pica, open	0	50
Double Pica,	0	50
Great Primer	0	50
Great Primer, open	0	50
Pica	0	56
Long Primer	0	64
Brevier	0	84

Greeks.

Pica	0	72
Long Primer	0	80
Bourgeois	0	92
Brevier	1	12

Antiques.

Eight line Pica	0	28
Four line Pica	0	32
Canon	0	32
Double Great Primer	0	40
Double Pica	0	44
Great Primer	0	50
Pica	0	56
Long Primer	0	64
Brevier	0	84
Minion	1	20
Nonpareil	1	50

Metal Furniture. 0 28

Shades.

Two line Brevier	1	00
Two line Brevier, Double	1	25
Two line Minion	1	00
Two line Nonpareil	1	25
Two line Nonpareil, Double	1	25
Two line Nonpareil Meridian	1	25
Two line Pearl	1	25
Brevier	1	50

Italians.

Twelve line Pica	0	28
Seven line Pica	0	28
Five line Pica	0	30
Double Pica	0	60
Two line Brevier	0	60
Two line Nonpareil	0	64

English Back Slope. 0 64

Ornamented, &c.

Twelve line Pica Ornamented	0	44
Eight line Pica Fluted	0	44
Eight line Pica Oak Leaf	0	44
Eight line Pica Ornamented	0	44
Six line Pica Ornamented	0	50
Five line Pica Ornamented	0	50

Superiors, &c.

Figures, Letters; Signs, Astronomical, &c. double the price of common letter.

Flowers.

Pica, and all larger	0	36

Smaller than Pica, price of common type.

Space Rules. . . . 1 25

Piece Fractions.

Pica	1	25
Small Pica	1	60
Long Primer	2	

Quotations. 0 30

Leads.

Six to a Pica, and thicker	0	30
Seven to a Pica	0	34
Eight to a Pica	0	40
Nine to a Pica	0	50
Ten to a Pica	0	66

Lottery Figures. 0 44

Brass Rule

From 12 cts. to 62¼ cts. per foot.

Old Type received in exchange for the above at 9 cents per pound.—Spanish and French Accents cast to all sizes.—Large Letter and Cuts cast in *Moulds* and *Matrices*, on *metal bodies*, and with the *exactness* of the smaller letter.—Printing Presses and Ink, Chases, Composing Sticks, Gallies, Cases and Stands, Furniture (metal and wood), Quoins, Bodkins, Candlesticks, Ball Stocks and Skins, Composition Rollers, Parchments, &c. of superior quality.

3

SIGNS,

CAST TO VARIOUS SIZES.

Zodiacal Signs.

♈ Aries.	♋ Cancer.	♎ Libra.	♑ Capricornus.
♉ Taurus.	♌ Leo.	♏ Scorpio.	♒ Aquarius.
♊ Gemini.	♍ Virgo.	♐ Sagittarius.	♓ Pisces.

Planetary Signs.

⊙ Sun.	♃ Jupiter.	☿ Mercury.	⚴ Pallas.
♄ Saturn.	♀ Venus.	♅ Uranus.	⚵ Juno.
♂ Mars.	⊕ Earth.	⚳ Ceres.	⚶ Vesta.
● Moon.			

Aspects.

○ New Moon.	☊ Dragon's Head.	△ Trine.
☽ First Quarter.	☋ Dragon's Tail.	□ Quartile.
● Full Moon.	☌ Conjunction.	✱ Sextile.
☾ Last Quarter.	☍ Opposition.	☉ Sun.

Physical Signs.

℞ Recipe. ℔ Pound. ℥ Ounce.

ʒ Drachm. ℈ Scruple.

Mathematical, Algebraical, and Geometrical Signs.

+	=	×	−	÷	⊏	⊐	□	△
∽	∷	∶	−:	∥	∟	∻	√	○
∠	▭	⊥	±	<	>	⟋	° ′	″

SIGNS, CAST ON A SQUARE NONPAREIL BODY.

+−=×∶∷⊹÷□△∠⊥▭∠‾√⊏⊐<−:∽±∟♀ ☉⊙♈♉□♋♌

♍♎♏♐♑♒♓♄♃♂⊕♀☿♅⚶⚵⚳○☾●☌☍⊖✱ ℞℔℔℥ʒ℈

Quousque tandem abutere, Catilina, patientia nostra? quamdiu nos etiam furor iste tuus eludet? quem ad finem sese effrenata jactabit audacia? nihilne te nocturnum præsidium palatii, nihil urbis vigiliæ, nihil timor populi, nihil consensus bonorum omnium, nihil hic munitissimus habendi senatus locus, nihil horum ora vultusque moverunt? patere tua consilia non sentis? constrictam jam omnium horum conscientia, teneri conjurationem tuam non vides? quid proxima, quid superiore nocte egeris, ubi fueris, quos convocaveris, quid consilii ceperis, quem nostrum ignorare arbitraris? O tempora, o mores! Senatus hoc intelligit, consul videt: hic tamen vivit. Vivit? imo vero etiam in senatum venit: fit publici consilii particeps: notat et designat oculis ad cædem unumquemque nostrum. Nos autem viri fortes satisfacere reipublicæ videmur, si istius furorem ac tela vitemus. Ad mortem te, Catilina, duci jussu consulis jam pridem oportebat: in te conferri pestem istam, quam tu in nos omnes jamdiu machinaris. An vero vir amplissimus, P. Scipio, pontifex maximus, Tiberium Gracchum mediocriter labefactantem statum reipublicæ privatus interfecit: Catilinam vero orbem

ABCDEFGHIJKLMNOPQRSTUVWXYZÆŒ

ABCDEFGHIJKLMNOPQRSTUVWXYZÆŒ

$ 1234567890 £

Quousque tandem abutere, Catilina, patientia nostra? quamdiu nos etiam furor iste tuus eludet? quem ad finem sese effrenata jactabit audacia? nihilne te nocturnum præsidium palatii, nihil urbis vigiliæ, nihil timor populi, nihil consensus bonorum omnium, nihil hic munitissimus habendi senatus locus, nihil horum ora vultusque moverunt? patere tua consilia non sentis? constrictam jam omnium horum conscientia teneri conjurationem tuam non vides? quid proxima, quid superiore nocte egeris, ubi fueris, quos convocaveris, quid consilii ceperis, quem nostrum ignorare arbitraris? O tempora, o mores! Senatus hoc intelligit, consul videt: hic tamen vivit. Vivit? imo vero etiam in senatum venit: fit publici consilii particeps: notat et designat oculis ad cædem unumquemque nostrum. Nos autem viri fortes satisfacere reipublicæ videmur, si istius furorem ac tela vitemus. Ad mortem te, Catilina, duci jussu consulis jam pridem oportebat: in te conferri pestem istam, quam tu in nos omnes jamdiu machinaris. An vero vir amplissimus, P. Scipio, pontifex maximus, Tiberium Gracchum mediocriter labefactantem statum reipublicæ privatus interfecit: Catilinam vero orbem terræ cæde atque incendiis vastare cupientem nos consules perferemus? nam illa nimis antiqua

ABCDEFGHIJKLMNOPQRSTUVWXYZÆŒ

5

Quousque tandem abutere, Catilina, patientia nostra?
quamdiu nos etiam furor iste tuus eludet? quem ad
finem sese effrenata jactabit audacia? nihilne te nocturnum præsidium palatii, nihil urbis vigiliæ, nihil timor
populi, nihil consensus bonorum omnium, nihil hic munitissimus habendi senatus locus, nihil horum ora vultusque
moverunt? patere tua consilia non sentis? constrictam
jam omnium horum conscientia teneri conjurationem
tuam non vides? quid proxima, quid superiore nocte
egeris, ubi fueris, quos convocaveris, quid consilii ceperis, quem nostrum ignorare arbitraris? O tempora, o
mores! Senatus hoc intelligit, consul videt: hic tamen
vivit. Vivit? imo vero etiam in senatum venit: fit publici consilii particeps: notat et designat oculis ad cædem
unumquemque nostrum. Nos autem viri fortes satisfacere reipublicæ videmur, si istius furorem ac tela vitemus. Ad mortem te, Catilina, duci jussu consulis jam
pridem oportebat: in te conferri pestem istam, quam tu
in nos omnes jamdiu machinaris. An vero vir amplissi-

ABCDEFGHIJKLMNOPQRSTUVWXYZÆŒ

ABCDEFGHIJKLMNOPQRSTUVWXYZÆŒ

$ 1234567890   £

Quousque tandem abutere, Catilina, patientia nostra?
quamdiu nos etiam furor iste tuus eludet? quem ad
finem sese effrenata jactabit audacia? nihilne te noctur-
num præsidium palatii, nihil urbis vigiliæ, nihil timor
populi, nihil consensus bonorum omnium, nihil hic mu-
nitissimus habendi senatus locus, nihil horum ora vul-
tusque moverunt? patere tua consilia non sentis? con-
strictam jam omnium horum conscientia teneri conjura-
tionem tuam non vides? quid proxima, quid superiore
nocte egeris, ubi fueris, quos convocaveris, quid consilii
ceperis, quem nostrum ignorare arbitraris? O tempora,
o mores! Senatus hoc intelligit, consul videt: hic tamen
vivit. Vivit? imo vero etiam in senatum venit: fit
publici consilii particeps: notat et designat oculis ad
cædem unumquemque nostrum. Nos autem viri fortes
satisfacere reipublicæ videmur, si istius furorem ac tela
vitemus. Ad mortem te, Catilina, duci jussu consulis
jam pridem oportebat: in te conferri pestem istam, quam
tu in nos omnes jamdiu machinaris. An vero vir am-

ABCDEFGHIJKLMNOPQRSTUVWXYZÆŒ

6

Quousque tandem abutere, Catilina, patientia
nostra? quamdiu nos etiam furor iste tuus eludet? quem ad finem sese effrenata jactabit audacia? nihilne te nocturnum præsidium palatii,
nihil urbis vigiliæ, nihil timor populi, nihil consensus bonorum omnium, nihil hic munitissimus
habendi senatus locus, nihil horum ora vultusque
moverunt? patere tua consilia non sentis? constrictam jam omnium horum conscientia teneri

ABCDEFGHIJKLMNOPQRSTUVWXYZÆ

ABCDEFGHIJKLMNOPQRSTUVWXYZÆŒ

§ 1234567890 ¹¹¹¹²³³⁵⁷⁄₂₃₄₈₃₄₈₈₈ £

Quousque tandem abutere, Catilina, patientia nostra? quamdiu nos etiam furor iste tuus eludet?
quem ad finem sese effrenata jactabit audacia?
nihilne te nocturnum præsidium palatii, nihil urbis
vigiliæ, nihil timor populi, nihil consensus bonorum
omnium, nihil hic munitissimus habendi senatus
locus, nihil horum ora vultusque moverunt? patere
tua consilia non sentis? constrictam jam omnium
horum conscientia teneri conjurationem tuam non

ABCDEFGHIJKLMNOPQRSTUVWXYZÆ

ABCDEFGHIJKLMNOPQRSTUVWXYZÆŒ

*Quousque tandem abutere, Catilina, patientia nos-
tra? quamdiu nos etiam furor iste tuus eludet?
quem ad finem sese effrenata jactabit audacia? nihilne te nocturnum præsidium palatii, nihil urbis
vigiliæ, nihil timor populi, nihil consensus bonorum
omnium, nihil hic munitissimus habendi senatus
locus, nihil horum ora vultusque moverunt? patere
tua consilia non sentis? constrictam jam omnium
horum conscientia teneri conjurationem tuam non*

ABCDEFGHIJKLMNOPQRSTUVWXYZÆ

Quousque tandem abutere, Catilina, patientia nostra? quamdiu nos etiam furor iste tuus eludet? quem ad finem sese effrenata jactabit audacia? nihilne te nocturnum præsidium palatii, nihil urbis vigiliæ, nihil timor populi, nihil consensus bonorum omnium, nihil hic munitissimus habendi senatus locus, nihil horum ora vultusque moverunt? patere tua consilia non sentis? constrictam jam omnium horum conscientia teneri conjurationem tuam non vides? quid proxima, quid superiore nocte egeris, ubi fueris, quos convocaveris, quid consilii ceperis, quem

ABCDEFGHIJKLMNOPQRSTUVWX

ABCDEFGHIJKLMNOPQRSTUVWXYZÆŒ

$ 1234567890 £

Quousque tandem abutere, Catilina, patientia nostra? quamdiu nos etiam furor iste tuus eludet? quem ad finem sese effrenata jactabit audacia? nihilne te nocturnum præsidium palatii, nihil urbis vigiliæ, nihil timor populi, nihil consensus bonorum omnium, nihil hic munitissimus habendi senatus locus, nihil horum ora vultusque moverunt? patere tua consilia non sentis? constrictam jam omnium horum conscientia teneri conjurationem tuam non vides? quid proxima, quid superiore nocte egeris, ubi fueris, quos convo-

ABCDEFGHIJKLMNOPQRSTUV WXYZÆŒ

Quousque tandem abutere, Catilina, patientia nostra? quamdiu nos etiam furor iste tuus eludet? quem ad finem sese effrenata jactabit audacia? nihilne te nocturnum præsidium palatii, nihil urbis vigiliæ, nihil timor populi, nihil consensus bonorum omnium, nihil hic munitissimus habendi senatus locus, nihil horum ora vultusque moverunt? patere tua consilia non sentis? constrictam jam omnium horum conscientia teneri conjurationem tuam non vides? quid proxima, quid superiore nocte egeris, ubi fueris, quos convocaveris, quid consilii ceperis, quem nostrum ignorare

ABCDEFGHIJKLMNOPQRSTUVWXY

ABCDEFGHIJKLMNOPQRSTUVWXYZÆŒ

$ 1234567890 £

Quousque tandem abutere, Catilina, patientia nostra? quamdiu nos etiam furor iste tuus eludet? quem ad finem sese effrenata jactabit audacia? nihilne te nocturnum præsidium palatii, nihil urbis vigiliæ, nihil timor populi, nihil consensus bonorum omnium, nihil hic munitissimus habendi senatus locus, nihil horum ora vultusque moverunt? patere tua consilia non sentis? constrictam jam omnium horum conscientia teneri conjurationem tuam non vides? quid proxima, quid superiore nocte egeris, ubi fueris, quos convocaveris, quid consilii ceperis, quem nostrum ignorare arbi-

ABCDEFGHIJKLMNOPQRSTUVW XYZÆŒ

Quousque tandem abutere, Catilina, patientia nostra? quamdiu nos etiam furor iste tuus eludet? quem ad finem sese effrenata jactabit audacia? nihilne te nocturnum præsidium palatii, nihil urbis vigiliæ, nihil timor populi, nihil consensus bonorum omnium, nihil hic muni-

ABCDEFGHIJKLMNOPQRSTUVWXYZÆŒ&

$ 1234567890 $\frac{2}{8}\frac{1}{4}\frac{3}{4}\frac{1}{8}$ £

Quousque tandem abutere, Catilina, patientia nostra? quamdiu nos etiam furor iste tuus eludet? quem ad finem sese effrenata jactabit audacia? nihilne te nocturnum præsidium palatii, nihil urbis vigiliæ, nihil timor populi, nihil consensus bonorum omnium, nihil hic muni-

ABCDEFGHIJKLMNOPQRSTUVWXYZÆŒ
AKMNUVWXY.

Quousque tandem abutere, Catilina, patientia nostra? quamdiu nos etiam furor iste tuus eludet? quem ad finem sese effrenata jactabit audacia? nihilne te nocturnum praesidium palatii, nihil urbis vigiliae, nihil timor populi, nihil consensus bonorum om-

ABCDEFGHIJKLMNOPQRSTUVWXYZÆŒ

ABCDEFGHIJKLMNOPQRSTUVWXYZÆŒ

$ 1234567890 £

Quousque tandem abutere, Catilina, patientia nostra? quamdiu nos etiam furor iste tuus eludet? quem ad finem sese effrenata jactabit audacia? nihilne te nocturnum praesidium palatii, nihil urbis vigiliae, nihil timor populi, nihil consensus bonorum omnium, nihil

ABCDEFGHIJKLMNOPQRSTUVWXYZÆŒ

11

DOUBLE PICA.

Quousque tandem abutere, Catilina, patientia nostra? quamdiu nos etiam furor iste tuus eludet? quem ad finem sese effrenata jactabit audacia? ni-
ABCDEFGHIJKLMNOPQRSTUVWXYZ
$ 1234567890 £

Quousque tandem abutere, Catilina, patientia nostra? quamdiu nos etiam furor iste tuus eludet? quem ad finem sese effrenata jactabit au-
ABCDEFGHIJKLMNOPQRSTUVW
AMNUVWY.

REAL DOUBLE PICA.

Quousque tandem abutere, Catilina, patientia nostra? quamdiu nos etiam furor iste tuus eludet? quem ad finem sese efABCDEFGHIJKLMNOPQRSTUVW
$ 1234567890 $

Quousque tandem abutere, Catilina, patientia nostra? quamdiu nos etiam furor iste tuus eludet? quem ad finem ABCDEFGHIJKLMNOPQRSTU

Quousque tandem abutere, Catilina, patientia nostra? quamdiu nos etiam furor
iste tuus eludet? quem ad finem sese
effrenata jactabit audacia? nihilne te
nocturnum præsidium palatii, nihil urbis vigiliæ, nihil timor populi, nihil con-
ABCDEFGHIJKLMNOPQRSTUV

$ 1234567890 £

14

Quousque tandem abutere, Catilina,
patientia nostra? quamdiu nos etiam
furor iste tuus eludet? quem ad finem
sese effrenata jactabit audacia? nihilne te nocturnum praesidium palatii,
nihil urbis vigiliae, nihil timor populi

ABCDEFGHIJKLMNOPQRSTU
VWXYZÆŒ

15

Quousque tandem abutere, Catilina, patientia nostra? quamdiu nos etiam furor iste tuus eludet? quem ad finem sese effrenata jactabit audacia? nihilne te nocturnum præsidium palatii, nihil urbis vigiliæ, nihil timor

ABCDEFGHIJKLMNOPQRSTU

$ 1234567890 £

Quousque tandem abutere, Catilí-
na, patientia nostra? quamdiu nos
etiam furor iste tuus eludet? quem
ad finem sese effrenata jactabit
audacia? nihilne te nocturnum
præsidium palatii, nihil urbis vi-

ABCDEFGHIJKLMNOPQRS
TUVWXYZÆŒ

17

Quousque tandem abutere,
Catilina, patientia nostra?
quamdiu nos etiam furor iste tuus eludet? quem ad finem sese effrenata jactabit
ABCDEFGHIJKLMNOP
$ 1234567890 £
$

18

Quousque tandem abutere, Catilina, patientia nostra? quamdiu nos etiam furor iste tuus eludet? quem ad fi- nem sese effrenata jactabit

ABCDEFGHIJKLMN OPQRSTUVWXYZ

19

Quousque tandem abute
re, Catilina, patientia no
stra? quamdiu nos etiam

ABCDEFGHIJKLMN

$ 1234567890 £

DOUBLE PARAGON.

Quousque tandem abute-
re, Catilina, patientia nostra? quamdiu nos etiam

ABCDEFGHIJKLM
AK.MNUVWXYÆ

Quousque tandem abu
tere Catilina, patientia
nostra? quamdiu nos
ABCDEFGHIJKLM
$ 1234567890)

Quousque tandem ab utere, Catilina, pati entia nostra? quam-

ABCDEFGHIJKL
MNOPQRSTUVW

Quousque tandem abutere, Catilina, patientia nostra? qu

ABCDEFGHIJK

$ 1234567890 £

Quousque tandem
abutere, Catilina,
patientia nostra?
ABCDEGHIJK
LMNOPQRSUV

25

ABCDEFGH

Manchester.

$1234567&

Metamora

ABCDE

A.M.Y.

GREAT PRIMER, No. 3. CONDENSED.

ABCDEFGHIJKLMNOPQRSTUVWXYZ& , . - ' CONDENSED.

27

Metamora

ABCDE
ABCDE

CDE

GREAT PRIMER, No. 3. CONDENSED.

ABCDEFGHIJKLMNOPQRSTUVWXYZ& , . - '   CONDENSED.

28

FOURTEEN LINES PICA.

TWENTY LINES PICA.

TWENTY LINES PICA.

How far, O Catiline, wilt thou abuse our patience? How long shall thy frantic rage baffle the efforts of justice? To what height meanest thou to carry thy daring insolence? Art thou nothing daunted by the nocturnal watch posted to secure the Palatium? nothing by the city guards? nothing by the consternation of the people? nothing by the union of all the wise and worthy citizens? nothing by the senate's assembling in this place of strength? nothing by the looks and countenances of all here present? Se st thou not that all thy designs are brought to light? that the senators are

Quousque tandem abutere, Catilina, patientia nostra? quamdiu nos etiam furor iste tuus eludet? quem ad finem sese effrenata jactabit audacia? nihilne te nocturnum præsidium palatii, nihil urbis vigiliæ, nihil timor populi, nihil consensus bonorum omnium, nihil hic munitissimus habendi senatus locus, nihil horum ora vultusque moverunt? patere tua consilia non sentis? constrictam jam omnium horum conscientia teneri conjurationem tuam non vides? quid proxima, quid superiore nocte egeris, ubi fueris, quos convocaveris, quid consilii ceperis, quem nostrum ignorare arbitraris? O tempora, o

ABCDEFGHIJKLMNOPQRSTUVWX
YZÆŒ 1234567890 $

ΕΔΕΙ μέν, ὦ ἄνδρες Ἀθηναῖοι, τοὺς, λέγοντας ἅπαντας ἐν ὑμῖν, μήτε πρὸς ἔχθραν ποιεῖσθαι λόγον μηδένα, μήτε πρὸς χάριν. ἀλλ᾽ ὅ βέλτιςον ἕκαστος ἡγειτο, τοῦτ᾽ ἀποφαίνεσθαι. ἄλλως τε καὶ πὲρὶ κοινῶν πραγμάτον καὶ μεγάλων ὑμῶν βϑλευομένων, ἐπειδὴ δὲ νεοιν τὰ μὲν, φιλονεικίᾳ, τὰ δὲ ἧ τινι δήποτ᾽ αἰτίᾳ, προάγονται λέγειι, ὑμᾶς, ὦ ἄνδρες Ἀθηναῖοι, τοὺς πολλοὺς δεῖ, πάντα τἄλλ᾽ ἀφέντας, ἃ τῇ πόλει νομίζετε συμφέρειν, ταῦτ καὶ ψηφίζεσθαι καὶ πραττειν. ἡ μεν οῶν σπϑδὴ, περὶ τῶν ἐν Χεῤῥονήσῳ πραγμάτων ἐστὶ, καὶ τῆς ςρατείας, ἣν ἐνδέκατον μῆνα τουτονὶ, Φίλιππος ἐν Θράκη ποιεῖται. τῶν δὲ λόγων οἱ πλεῖστοι, περὶ ὧν Διοπείθης πράττει καὶ μέλλει ποιεῖν, εἰρηνται.

ΑΒΓΔΕΖΗΘΙΚΛΜΝΞΟΠΡΣΤΥΦΧΨΩ

Long Primer Greek.

Τοῦτον τὸν Ἀρίονα λέγουσι, τὸν πολλὸν τοῦ χρόνου διατρίβοντα παρα Περιανδρῳ, επιθυμησαι πλωσαι ες Ιταλιην τε και Σικηλιην· εργασαμενον ϱου χρηματα μεγαλα, θελησαι απισω ες Κορινθον απικεσθαι. Ορμασθαι μϑν νυν εκ Ταραντος, πιστευοντα δε ουδαμοισι μαλλον η Κορινθιοισι, μισθωσασθαι πλοιον ανδϱων Κορινθιων. Τους δε, εν τω πελαγει, επιβουλευειν, τον Αριονα εκβαλοντας, ουχειν τα χρηματα. Τον δε, συνεντα τουτο, λισσεσθαι χρηματα μεν προιεντα σφι, ψυχην δε παραιτεομεϰον. Ουκων δη πειθϑιν αυτον τουτοισι, αλλα κελευειν τους πορθμεας η αυτον διαχϱασθαι μιν, ως αν ταφης εν γη τυχη, η εκπηδαν ες την θαλασσαν την ταχιστην. Απειληθεντα δε τον Αριονα ες απορινην, παραιτησασθαι, επειδη σφι ουτω δοκεοι, περιδεειν αυτον, εν τη σκευη παση, σταντα εν τοιϱι εδωλιοισι, αεισαι· αεισας δε, υπεδεκετο εωυτον κατεργα

Pica Greek.

ΕΔΕΙ μέν, ὦ ἄνδρες Ἀθηναῖοι, τοὺς, λέγοντας ἅπαντας ἐν ὑμῖν, μήτε ϱός ἔχϑραν ποιεῖσθαιν λόγον μηδένα, μήτε πρὸς χάριν. ἀλλ᾽ ὅ βέλτιςοὶ ἕκαςος ἡγειτο, τοῦτ ἀποφαίνεσθαι. ἄλλως τε καπὲρὶ κοινῶν πραγμάτον καὶ μεγάλων ὑμῶν βϑλευομένων, ἐπειδὴ δὲ νεοιν τὰ μὲν, φιλονεικίᾳ, τὰ δὲ ἧ τινι δήποτ αἰτίᾳ, προάγονται λέγειι, ὑμᾶς, ὦ ἄνδρες Ἀθηναῖοι, τοὺς πολλοὺς δεῖ, πάντα τἄλλ ἀφέντας, ἃ τῇ πόλει νομίζετε συμφέρειν, ταῦτ καὶ ψηφίζεσθαι καὶ πραττειν. ἡ μεν οῶν σπϑδὴ, περὶ τῶν ἐν Χεῤῥονήσῳ πραγμάτων ἐςὶ, καὶ τῆϛ

ΑΒΓΔΕΖΗΘΙΚΛΜΝΞΟΠΡΤΥΦΧΨΩ

34

ABCDEFGHIJKLMNOPQRSTUV
WXYZÆŒ.,;:!?- $ 1234567890 £

ABCDEFGHIJKLMNOPQRSTU
VWXYZ.,;:!? $ 1234567890 £

ABCDEFGHIJKLMNOPQRSTUVW
XYZÆŒ&.,;:?-

35

ABCDEFGHIJKLMNOPQRSTUVWXY
ZÆŒ&.,;:?-

TWO LINES BOURGEOIS, No. 1.

ABCDEFGHIJKLMNOPQRSTUVWXYZÆŒ
&.,;:?- $ 1234567890 £

TWO LINES BOURGEOIS, No. 2.

ABCDEFGHIJKLMNOPQRSTUVWXYZÆŒ
.,;:!?- $ 1234567890 £

TWO LINES BREVIER, No. 1.

ABCDEFGHIJKLMNOPQRSTUVWXYZÆŒ&.,;:?-
$ 1234567890 £

36

TWO LINES BREVIER, No. 2.

ABCDEFGHIJKLMNOPQRSTUVWXYZ&.,;:!?'
$ 1234567890 £

TWO LINES MINION.

ABCDEFGHIJKLMNOPQRSTUVWXYZ&ÆŒ.,;:!?-
$ 1234567890 £

TWO LINES NONPAREIL. No. 1.

ABCDEFGHIJKLMNOPQRSTUVWXYZÆŒ&.,;:!?-
$ 1234567890 £

TWO LINES NONPAREIL, No. 2.

ABCDEFGHIJKLMNOPQRSTUVWXYZ
& ÆŒ 1234567890 £ .,;:-?!¿

37

TWO LINE BREVIER, TITLE LETTER.

ABCDEFGHIJKLMNOPQRSTUVWXYZÆŒ&.,;:'-

TWO LINE MINION, TITLE LETTER.

ABCDEFGHIJKLMNOPQRSTUVWXYZÆŒ&.,;:'-

TWO LINE NONPAREIL, TITLE LETTER.

ABCDEFGHIJKLMNOPQRSTUVWXYZÆŒ&.,;:'-

SPACE RULE.

1 n	1 m	2 m	3 m	4 m	5 m	6 m
—	—	—	—	—	—	—

38

Long Primer Roman, No. 4.

How far, O Catiline, wilt thou abuse our patience? How long shall thy frantic rage baffle the efforts of justice? To what height meanest thou to carry thy daring insolence? Art thou nothing daunted by the nocturnal watch posted to secure the Palatium? nothing by the city guards? nothing by the consternation of the people? nothing by the union of all the wise and worthy citizens? nothing by the senate's assembling in this place of strength?

ABCDEFGHIJKLMNOPQRSTUVWXYZ

[$ 1234567890 $]

Long Primer Italic, No. 4.

How far, O Catiline, wilt thou abuse our patience? How long shall thy frantic rage baffle the efforts of justice? To what height meanest thou to carry thy daring insolence? Art thou nothing daunted by the nocturnal watch posted to secure the Palatium? nothing by the city guards? nothing by the consternation of the people? nothing by the union of all the wise and worthy citizens? nothing by the senate's assembling in this place of strength?

ABCDEFGHIJKLMNOPQRSTUVW

Minion Full Face.

How far, O Catiline, wilt thou abuse our patience? How long shall thy frantic rage baffle the efforts of justice? To what height meanest thou to carry thy daring insolence? Art thou nothing daunted by the nocturnal watch posted to secure the Palatium? nothing by the city guards? nothing by the consternation of the people? nothing by the union of all the wise and worthy citizens? nothing by the senate's assembling in this place of strength? nothing by the looks and countenances of all here present? Seest thou not that all thy designs are brought to light? that the senators are not ignorant of

ABCDEFGHIJKLMNOPQRSTUVWXYZ&

[$ 1234567890 $]

39

40

TWO LINES PEARL.

ABCDEFGHIJKLMNOPQRSTUVWXYZ&.,;:!?- $ 1234567890 £

ENGLISH BLACK GROUND.

1234567890123456789012345678901234567890

SMALL PICA BLACK GROUND.

235678909999999999676682998837635568676687 | | | |

SHADED TWO LINE MINION ITALIC.

QUOUSQUE TANDEM ABUTERE CATILINA,
1234567890 ÆŒ & $ £ ,,,,,,,,,,,,,,,ffffffffffff

TWO LINE PEARL ROMAN SHADE.

ABCDEFGHIJKLMNOPQRSTUVWXYZÆŒ1234567890,,,,,,,,,,,ffff$

SHADED TWO LINE PEARL ITALIC.

ABCDEFGHIJKLMNOPQRSTUVWXYZ&ÆŒ,,,,,,,,,,,,ffff$1234567890

41

BREVIER TUSCAN SHADE.

ABCDEFGHIJKLMNOPQRSTUVWXYZ&ÆŒ.,:;

LONG PRIMER MERIDIAN SHADE.

ABCDEFGHIJKLMNOPQRSTUVWXYZ&ÆŒ.,:;

LONG PRIMER GOTHIC.

ABCDEFGHIJKLMNOPQRSTUVWXYZ,;:-'!

GREAT PRIMER CONDENSED.

ABCDEFGHIJKLMNOPQRSTUVWXYZ&,.'

PEARL BORDER, No. 1.

PEARL BORDER, No. 2.

SIX LINE BORDER, No. 4.

42

TWO LINES BREVIER SHADE.

ABCDEFGHIJKLMNOPQRSTUVWXYZ
ÆŒ&.,;;!?'-

TWO LINES BREVIER DOUBLE SHADE.

ABCDEFGHIJKLMNOPQRSTUVWXYZ,.,;:!?'-
& 1234567890 Q

TWO LINES NONPAREIL DOUBLE SHADE.

ABCDEFGHIJKLMNOPQRSTUVWXYZÆŒ&.,;:!?'-
& 1234567890 Æ

TWO LINES NONPAREIL MERIDIAN SHADE.

ABCDEFGHIJKLMNOPQRSTUVWXYZ.,;:!?'-
$ 1234567890 &

TWO LINES BREVIER ITALIAN.

ABCDEFGHIJKLMNOPQRSTUVWXYZ&.,;:!?
$ 1234567890

PICA ITALIAN.

ABCDEFGHIJKLMNOPQRSTUVWXYZ&.,;:!? $ 1234567890

PICA ANTIQUE.

ABCDEFGHIJKLMNOPQRSTUVWXYZ&.,;i!?'- $ 1234567890

LONG PRIMER ANTIQUE.

ABCDEFGHIJKLMNOPQRSTUVWXYZ&.,;i!?'- $ 1234567890

BREVIER ANTIQUE.

ABCDEFGHIJKLMNOPQRSTUVWXYZ&.,;i!?'- $ 1234567890

MINION ANTIQUE.

ABCDEFGHIJKLMNOPQRSTUVWXYZ&.,;i!?'- $ 1234567890

NONPAREIL ANTIQUE.

ABCDEFGHIJKLMNOPQRSTUVWXYZ.,;i!?'- $ 1234567890

44

GREAT PRIMER BLACK.

Quousque tandem abutere, Catilina, patientia nostra Quamdiu nos eti= am furor iste tuus eludet Quem ad finem sese effrenata factabit audacia

ABCDEFGHIJKLMNOPQRSTU abcdefghijklmnopqrstuvwxyz

BREVIER BLACK.

Quousque tandem abutere, Catilina, patientia nostra Quam diu nos etiam furor iste tuus eludet Quem ad finem sese effrenata factabit audacia Nihilne te nocturnum præsidum palatii nihil urbis bigilia, nihil timor populi, nihil consensus bo= norum omnium, nihil hic munitissimus habendi senatus locus, nihil horum ora bultusque moberunt Patere tuua consilia
ABCDEFGHIJKLMNOPQRSTUVWXYZ & abcdefghijklmnopqrstuvwxyz,;;:-'

PICA ANTIQUE.

Quousque tandem abutere, Catilina, patientia, nostra Quam diu nos etiam furor iste tuus eludet Quem ad finem sese

NONPAREIL FULL FACE.

Quousque tandem abutere, Catilina, patientia nostra; quamdiu nos etiam furor iste tuus eludet quem ad finem sese effrenata jactabit audacia? nihilne te nocturnum præsidium palatii, nihil urbis vigiliæ, nihil timor populi, nihil consensus bonorum omnium, nihil hic munitissimus habendi senatus locus, nihil horum ora vultusque moverunt? patere tua consilia non sentis? constrictam jam omnium horum conscientia,

To be Sold at Auction without reserh

MUSTANGS & KICKSHAWES.

To be Sold at Auction without reserve this day

PITCH, ROSIN & TURPENTINE.

We hold these truths to be self=evident: that all Men are created equal; that they are endowed by their Creator with certain unalienable rights; that among these are life, liberty, and the pursuit of happiness; that to secure these rights

ABCDEFGHIJKLMNOPQRSTUVWXYZ

We hold these truths to be self=evident: that all Men are created equal; that they are endowed by their Creator with certain unalienable rights; that among these are life, liberty, and the pursuit of happiness; that to secure these rights governments are instituted among men, deriving their just

ABCDEFGHIJKLMNOPQRSTUVWXYZ

GREAT PRIMER ANTIQUE.

The governor of Cuba published a proclamation on the 18th of April, prohibiting the importation of all books which oppose the Catholic religion, the royalty, rights, and prerogatives of the sovereign, or which, in any other manner, defend the rebellion of vassals or nations. The masters and owners of vessels,

ABCDEFGHIJKLMNOPQRSTUVWXY

$ 1234567890 &

DOUBLE PICA ANTIQUE.

Lucius Catiline was descended of an illustrious family; he was a man of great vigour, both of body and mind, but of a disposition extremely profligate and depraved. From his youth he took

ABCDEFGHIJKLMNOPQRST
$ 1234567890 &

48

Boston Type

ABCDEFGHIJ

123456

49

FOUR LINES PICA ANTIQUE.

JOHN ADAMS

T. JEFFERSON

$1234567890 &

Gazette.

Mercantile Lt

51

FIVE LINES PICA, OPEN BLACK.

United States.

FIVE LINES PICA BLACK.

Salem=Street, Boston.

FINE ARTS

PRESCOTT.

$1234567&

SIX LINES PICA ORNAMENTED.

MODERN

FANCY.

FIVE LINES PICA ORNAMENTED.

COLUMBIAN

SIX LINES PICA ORNAMENTED.   No. 2.

DURHAM

SIX LINES PICA ORNAMENTED.   No. 3.

MADISON

BOSTON!

$12345&3

57

EIGHT LINES PICA ANTIQUE.

TIMES!

24,56$!

EIGHT LINES PICA FLUTED.

TWELVE LINES PICA ORNAMENTED.

DOUBLE GREAT PRIMER ANTIQUE.

Aixlachapelle. SIX!

61

TWELVE LINES PICA ITALIAN.

BRHM
1234567890

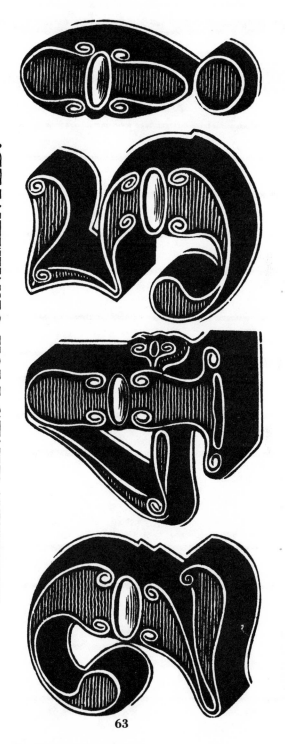

SIXTEEN LINES PICA ORNAMENTED.

63

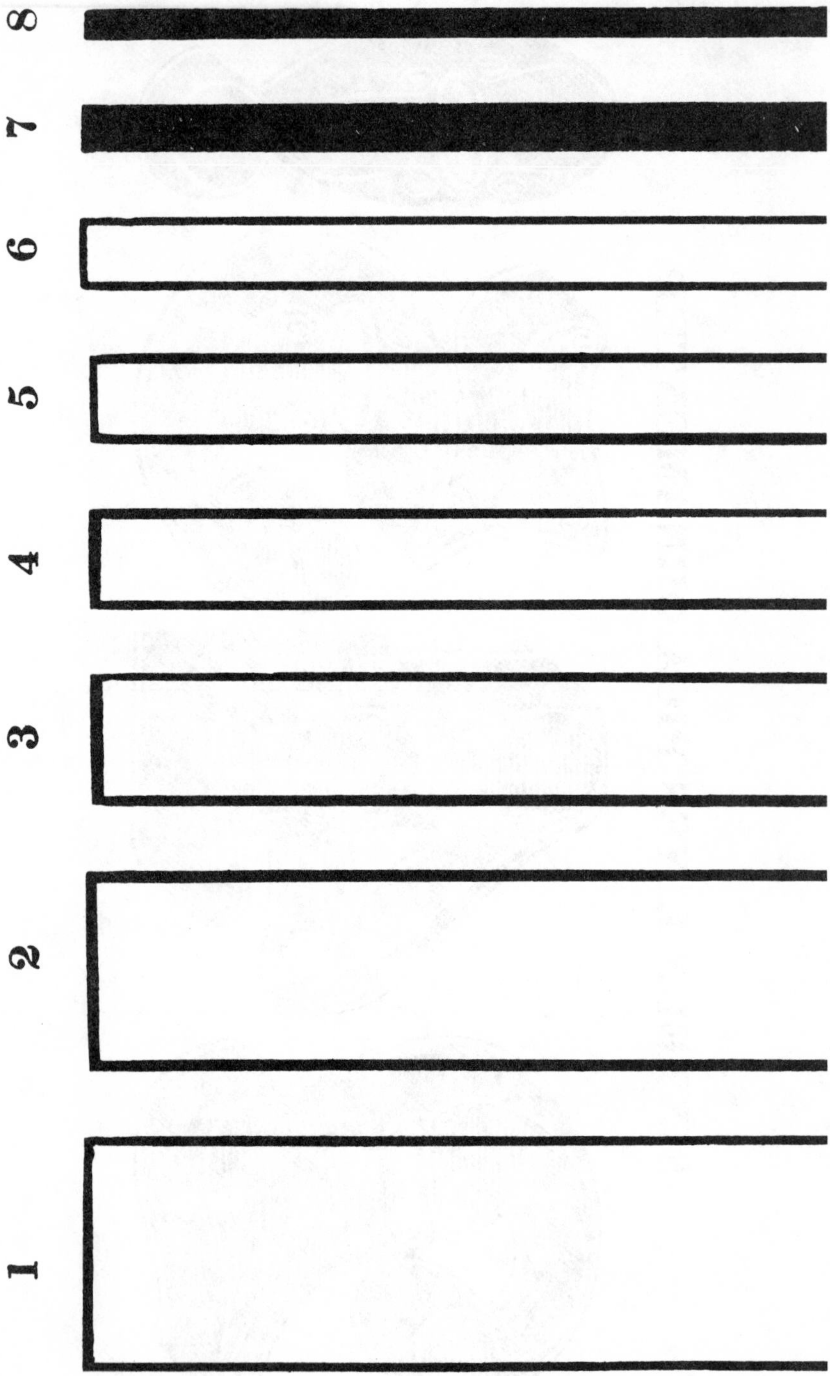
1
2
3
4
5
6
7
8

BRASS RULE.

No. 1.

No. 2.

No. 3.

No. 4.

No. 5.

No. 6.

No. 7.

No. 8.

No. 9.

No. 10.

No. 11.

No. 12.

No. 13.

BOSTON TYPE AND STEREOTYPE FOUNDRY.

DASHES.

DOUBLE ENGLISH.

Combination will produce three or four patterns of this dash.

PICA.

1
2
3
4
5
6
7

LONG PRIMER.

1   2   3   4   5
6   7   8
9   10
11
12   13
14   15
16   17   18   19   20

BOURGEOIS.

1   2   3   4
5   6   7
8   9

BREVIER.

1   2   3   4   5
6   7   8
9   10

MINION.

1   2   3   4   5
6   7   8   9

NONPAREIL.

NONPAREIL CHECK.

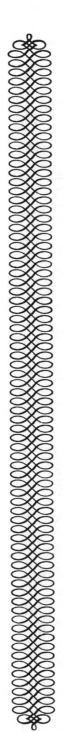

MINION CHECK.

DOUBLE ENGLISH CHECK.

DOUBLE ENGLISH OPEN CHECK.

67

FLOWERS AND BORDERS.

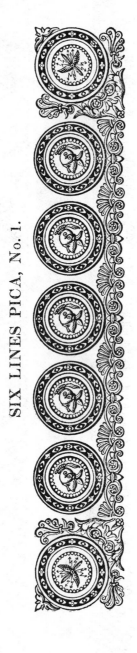

SIX LINES PICA, No. 1.

No. 2.

SIX LINES PICA, No. 3.

FIVE LINES PICA, No. 1.

No. 2.

69

FOUR LINES PICA, No. 1.

No. 2.

No. 3.

70

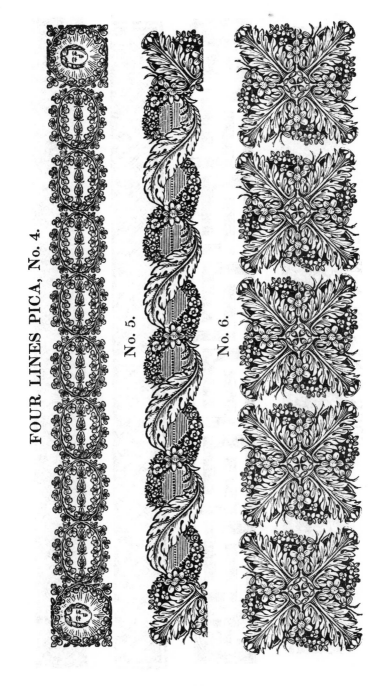

FOUR LINES PICA, No. 4.

No. 5.

No. 6.

71

FOUR LINES PICA, No. 7.

No. 8.

CANON, No. 1.

No. 2.

72

FOUR LINES PICA, No. 9.

FOUR LINES PICA, No. 10.

FOUR LINES PICA, No. 11.

73

CANON, No. 3.

No. 4.

No. 5.

DOUBLE GREAT PRIMER.

74

TWO LINES ENGLISH.

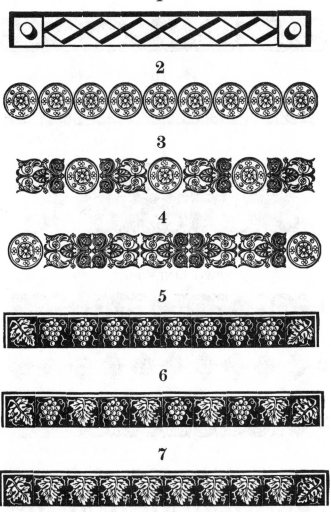

1

2

3

4

5

6

7

8

TWO LINES ENGLISH.

9

10

11

TWO LINES PICA.

1

2

3

DOUBLE PICA.

1

2

DOUBLE PICA

3

4

5

PARAGON.

1

2

GREAT PRIMER.

1

2

3

4

5

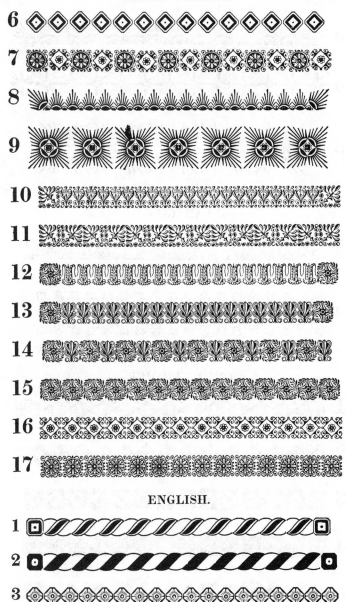

ENGLISH.

ENGLISH.

4
5
6
7
8
9
10
11
12

PICA.

1
2
3
4

5

6

7

8

9

10

11

12

13

14

15

16

17

18

19

SMALL PICA.

1
2
3
4
5
6
7
8
9

LONG PRIMER.

1
2
3
4
5
6
7

8

9

10

11

12

13

14

15

16

17

18

19

20

21

22

23

24

LONG PRIMER.

25

26

27

28

BOURGEOIS.

1

2

3

4

5

6

7

BREVIER.

1

2

3

4

5

6

7

8

9

10

11

12

13

BREVIER.

14

15

16

17

18

19

20

21

MINION.

1

2

3

4

5

6

7

8

9

10

11

12

13

MINION.

14 ✳~~~~~~~~~~~~~~~~~~~~~~~~~~✳

15 ⊞◇◇◇◇◇◇◇◇◇◇◇◇◇◇◇◇◇◇◇◇◇◇◇◇◇◇◇◇◇◇◇◇◇◇◇◇◇⊞

16 ⊞~~~~~~~~~~~~~~~~~~~~~~~~~~~⊞

17 ◇◆◇◆◇◆◇◆◇◆◇◆◇◆◇◆◇◆◇◆◇◆◇◆◇◆◇

18 ✳〉◇〈◇〉◇〈◇〉◇〈◇〉◇〈◇〉◇〈◇〉◇〈◇〉◇〈◇〉◇〈◇〉◇〈◇〉◇〈◇✳

19 ✳✳✳✳✳✳✳✳✳✳✳✳✳✳✳✳✳✳✳✳✳✳✳✳✳✳✳✳✳✳✳✳✳✳✳✳✳✳✳

NONPAREIL.

1 ⊞✕✳⊞

2 ⊞✳✳⊞

3 ✳╼╼╼╼╼╼╼╼╼╼╼╼╼╼╼╼╼╼╼╼╼╼╼╼╼╼╼╼╼╼╼╼╼╼╼╼╼✳

4 ✳∞∞∞∞∞∞∞∞∞∞∞∞∞∞∞∞∞∞∞∞∞∞∞∞∞∞∞∞∞∞∞∞∞✳

5 ⊞◇◇◇◇◇◇◇◇◇◇◇◇◇◇◇◇◇◇◇◇◇◇◇◇◇◇◇◇◇◇◇◇◇◇◇⊞

6 ✳∞∞∞∞∞∞∞∞∞∞∞∞∞∞∞∞∞∞∞∞∞∞∞∞∞∞∞∞∞∞∞∞✳

7 ✳ºº ✳

8 ⊡⊡⊡⊡⊡⊡⊡⊡⊡⊡⊡⊡⊡⊡⊡⊡⊡⊡⊡⊡⊡⊡⊡⊡⊡⊡⊡⊡⊡⊡⊡⊡⊡⊡⊡⊡⊡⊡⊡

9 ✳⬤⬤⬤⬤⬤⬤⬤⬤⬤⬤⬤⬤⬤⬤⬤⬤⬤⬤⬤⬤⬤⬤⬤⬤⬤⬤⬤⬤

10 ◇◇◇◇◇◇◇◇◇◇◇◇◇◇◇◇◇◇◇◇◇◇◇◇◇◇◇◇◇◇◇◇◇◇

11 ✳✳✳✳✳✳✳✳✳✳✳✳✳✳✳✳✳✳✳✳✳✳✳✳✳✳✳✳✳✳✳✳✳✳✳✳✳✳✳

NEWSPAPER ORNAMENTS.

GREAT PRIMER.
6 cents each.

DOUBLE PICA.
6 cents each.

TWO LINES ENGLISH.
8 cents.

TWO LINES GREAT PRIMER.
10 cents each.

1	2	3	4	5
6	7	8	9	10
11	12	13	14
15	16	17	18
19	20	21	CANON.

METAL ORNAMENTS.

No. 1.   37 cts.

No. 2.   50 cts.

No. 3.   37 cts.

No. 4.   25 cts.

No. 5.   37 cts.

No. 6.   75 cts.

No. 7.   50 cts.

No. 8.   87 cts.

No. 9.   50 cts.

No. 10.   87 cts.

No. 11.   87 cts.

No. 12.　87 cts.

No. 13.　50 cts.

No. 14.　75 cts.

No. 15.　87 cts.

No. 16.　$1.

No. 17.　50 cts.

No. 18.　75 cts.

No. 19.　25 cts.

No. 20.　50 cts.

No. 21.　50 cts.

No. 22.　37 cts.

No. 23.   75 cts.

No. 24. $1.

No. 25. $1.

No. 26. $1.50.

No. 27.   75 cts.

No. 28.   37 cts.

No. 29. $1.25.

No. 30. $1.25.

No. 31. $1.75.

No. 32. $2.

No. 33. $2.25.

No. 34. $1.75.

No. 35.   50 cts.   No. 36.   37 cts.

No. 37. $1.75.

No. 38. $1.12.

No. 39. 62 cts.

No. 41. $1.25.

No. 40. 50 cts.

No. 42. 62 cts.

No. 43. 50 cts.

No. 45. 50 cts.

No. 44. 37 cts.

93

No. 46. $1.12.

No. 47.   50 cts.

No. 48.   50 cts.

No. 49.   87 cts.

No. 50.   87 cts.

No. 51.   75 cts.

No. 52.   87 cts.

No. 53.   75 cts.

No. 54. 37 cts.

No. 55. 25 cts.

No. 56. 75 cts

No. 57. 87 cts.

No. 58. $1.

No. 59. 87 cts.

No. 61. 75 cts.

No. 60. 37 cts.

No. 62. 75 cts.

No. 63. 62 cts.

No. 64. $2.25

No. 65.   87 cts.

No. 66.   62 cts.

No 68.   87 cts.

No. 67.   50 cts.

No. 69.   87 cts.

No. 70.   75 cts.

No. 71.   75 cts.

No. 72.   50 cts.

No 73.   37 cts.

No. 74. $1.

No. 75.   50 cts.

No. 76.   62 cts.

No. 77.   50 cts.

No. 78.   50 cts.

No. 79. $1.

No. 80.   75 cts.

No. 82.   37 cts.

No. 83. $1.

No. 85. 75 cts.

No. 84.   50 cts.

No. 86. $2.25.

No. 87. $1.

No. 88.   25 cts.

No. 89. $2.

No. 90. $2.

No. 91. $1.25.

No. 93. 87 cts.

No. 92. 25 cts.

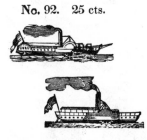

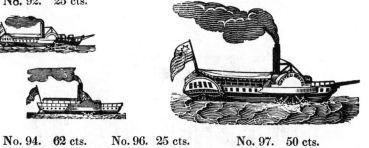

No. 94. 62 cts.   No. 96. 25 cts.   No. 97. 50 cts.

No. 98.   50 cts.

No. 99.   37 cts.

No. 100.   75 cts.

No. 101.   75 cts.

No. 102.   50 cts.

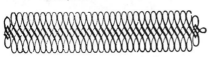

No. 103.   25 cts.   No. 104.   25 cts.

No. 105.

$1.

No. 107.   50 cts.

No. 106.   75 cts.

No. 108. $1.

No. 109. $1.12.

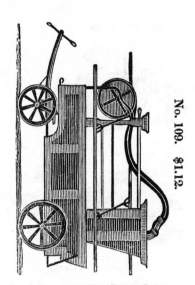

No. 110. 37 cts.   No. 111. 37 cts.   No. 112. 37 cts.

No. 113. $1.

No. 114. 75 cts.

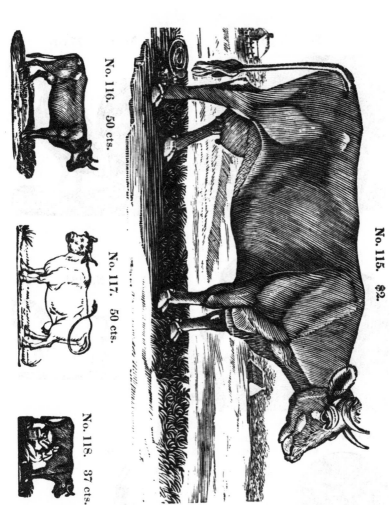

No. 115. $2.

No. 116. 50 cts.

No. 117. 50 cts.

No. 118. 37 cts.

No. 119. 75 cts.

No. 120. 75 cts.

No. 121. $1.

No. 123. 75 cts.

No. 122. $1.

No. 124. 50 cts.

No. 125. 50 cts.

No. 126. $1.

No. 127. 37 cts.

104

No. 129. $1.50.

No. 130.   50 cts.

No. 131. $1.25.

No. 132. $1.25.

No. 133. $1.25.

No. 134. $1.25.

No. 136. 50 cts.

No. 137. 50 cts.

No. 138. $1.25.

No. 140. $1.25.

No. 139. $1.25.

No. 141. $1.25.

No. 142. 50 cts.

No. 143. 50 cts.

No. 147. $1.25.

No. 144. $1.25

No. 148. $1.25.

No. 145. 50 cts.

No. 149. $1.12.

No. 146. 50 cts.

108

No. 153. $1.

No. 150.   50 cts.

No. 154. $1.12.

No. 151.   50 cts.

No. 155. $1.

No. 152.   50 cts.

109

No. 156.   50 cts.　　　　No. 157.   50 cts.

No. 158.   50 cts.　　　　No. 159.   50 cts.

No. 160.   50 cts.　　　　No. 161.   50 cts.

No. 162.   50 cts.　　　　No. 163.   50 cts.

No. 164.   50 cts.   No. 165.   50 cts.

No. 166.   50 cts.   No. 167.   50 cts.

No. 168.   50 cts.   No. 169.   50 cts

No. 170.   50 cts.   No. 171.   50 cts.

No. 172.   50 cts.   No. 173.   50 cts.

No. 174.   50 cts.   No. 175.   50 cts.

No. 176.   50 cts.   No. 177.   50 cts.

No. 178.   50 cts.   No. 179.   50 cts.

No. 180.   50 cts.

No. 181.   50 cts.

No. 182.   50 cts.

No. 183.   50 cts.

No. 184.   50 cts.

No. 185.   50 cts.

No. 186.   50 cts.

No. 187.   50 cts.

No. 188.   50 cts.   No. 189.   50 cts.

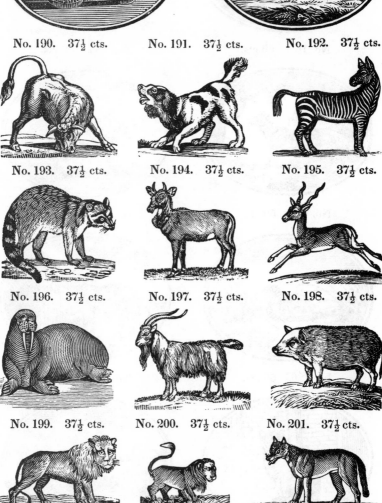

No. 190.   37½ cts.   No. 191.   37½ cts.   No. 192.   37½ cts.

No. 193.   37½ cts.   No. 194.   37½ cts.   No. 195.   37½ cts.

No. 196.   37½ cts.   No. 197.   37½ cts.   No. 198.   37½ cts.

No. 199.   37½ cts.   No. 200.   37½ cts.   No. 201.   37½ cts.

No. 202.   37½ cts.   No. 203.   37½ cts.   No. 204.   37½ cts.

No. 205.   37½ cts.   No. 206.   37½ cts.   No. 207.   37½ cts.

No. 208.   37½ cts.   No. 209.   37½ cts.   No. 210.   37½ cts

No. 211.   37½ cts.   No. 212.   37½ cts.   No. 213.   37½ cts.

No. 214.   37½ cts.   No. 215.   37½ cts.   No. 216.   37½ cts.

No. 217. $4.50.

No. 218. $3.50.

No. 219. $5.

No. 220. $3.50.

117

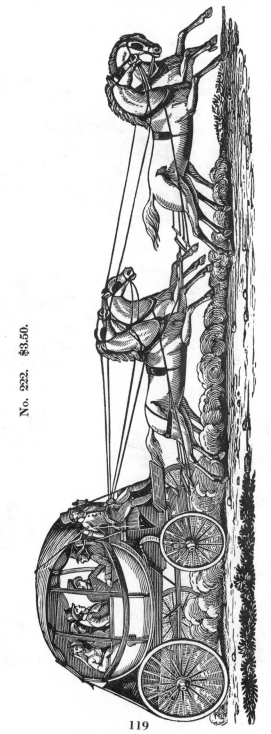

No. 222. $3.50.

119

No. 223. $1.75.

No. 224.   75 cts.

No. 225.   75 cts.

No. 226.   75 cts.

No. 227.   25 cts.

No. 229.   25 cts.

No. 228.   87 cts.

No. 230.   25 cts.

No. 231. $1.

WASHINGTON.

No. 232.   50 cts.

No. 233.   25 cts.

No. 234. $1.

No. 235.   25. cts.

No. 236. $1

No. 237.   62 cts.

No. 238.　$1.

No. 239.　75 cts.

No. 240.　37 cts.

No. 241.　75 cts.

No. 242.　37 cts.

No. 243.　$1.

No. 244.　50 cts.

No. 245. $1.

No. 246. 87 cts.

No. 247. 75 cts.

No. 248. 75 cts.

No. 249. 75 cts.

No. 250. $1.25.

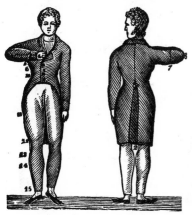

No. 251. $1.

Fashionable **CORSETS**

No. 252.　87 cts.

No. 253.　25 cts.

No. 254.　25 cts.

No. 255.　50 cts.

No. 256.　37 cts.

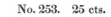

No. 257.　50 cts.

No. 259.　62 cts.

No. 258.　50 cts.

No. 260.　37 cts.

No. 261.　25 cts.

No. 262.　37 cts.

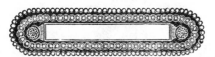

No. 263.　25 cts.

No. 264.　75 cts.

No. 265.　50 cts.

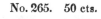

No. 266.　50 cts

No. 267.　50 cts.

No. 268.　50 cts.

No. 269.　50 cts.

No. 271.　25 cts

No. 270.　18 cts.

No. 272.　37 cts.

No. 273.　50 cts.

No. 274.　37 cts.

No. 275.　37 cts.

No. 276. $2.

BOSTON

TYPE AND STEREOTYPE

FOUNDRY.

No. 277. $1.12.

No. 278.   50 cts.

No. 279.   25 cts.

No. 280.   37 cts.

No. 281.   25 cts.

No. 282.   37 cts.

No. 282.　$1.12.

No. 284.　37 cts.

No. 285.　62 cts.

No. 286.　75 cts.

No. 287.　50 cts.

No. 288.　50 cts.

No. 289. 37 cts.

No. 291.　50 cts.

No. 290. 37 cts.

No. 292.　37 cts.

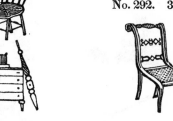

No. 293.　25 cts.

No. 294.　25 cts.

No. 295.　37 cts.

The following Cuts are twelve and a half cents each.

No. 296.   No. 297.   No. 298.

No. 299.   No. 300.   No. 301.

No. 302.   No. 303.   No. 304.

No. 305.   No. 306.   No. 307.

No. 308.   No. 309.   No. 310.

No. 311.   No. 312.   No. 313.

No. 314.   No. 315.   No. 316.

No. 317.   No. 318.   No. 319

No. 320. $1.25.

No. 321. $1.50.

No. 322. $1.50.

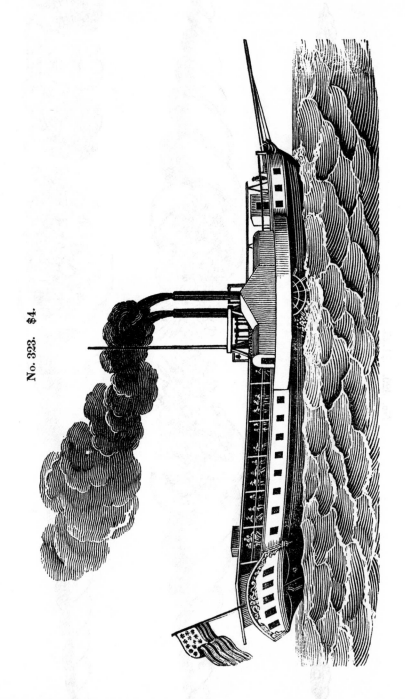

No. 323. $4.

130

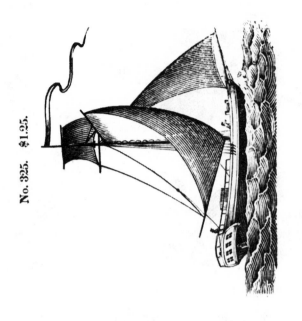

No. 325. $1.25.

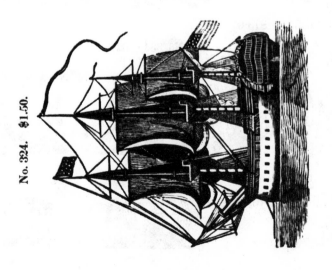

No. 324. $1.50.

No. 326.　87 cts.   No. 327.　37 cts.

No. 328.　87 cts.   No. 329.　50 cts.

No. 330.　37 cts.   No. 331.　50 cts.

No. 332.　37 cts.

No. 333.　87 cts.

No. 334.　62 cts.

No. 335.　50 cts.

No. 336. 25 cts.   No. 337.　25 cts.   No. 338.　10 cts.

No. 339. $1.

No. 340.   62 cts.

No. 341.   75 cts.

No. 342.   37 cts.

No. 343.   75 cts.

No. 344. $1

No. 345. $1.12.

No. 346.   75 cts.

No. 347.   37 cts.

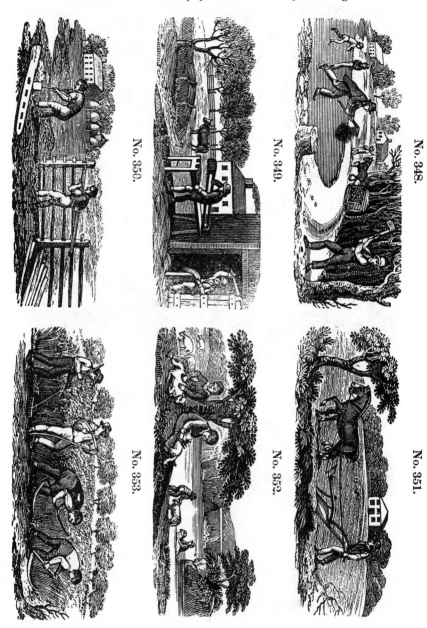

No. 348.

No. 349.

No. 350.

No. 351.

No. 352.

No. 353.

No. 354.

No. 355.

No. 356.

No. 357.

No. 358.

No. 359.

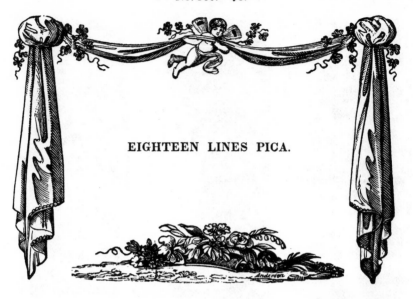

No. 360. $3.

EIGHTEEN LINES PICA.

No. 361. 87 cts.

No. 362. 75 cts.

No. 364. 87 cts.

No. 363. 75 cts.

No. 365. $1. No. 366. 50 cts. No. 367. $1.

No. 368. 50 cts.

No. 369. 50 cts.

No. 370. 37½ cts.   No. 371. 37½ cts.

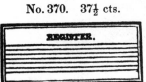

REGISTER.

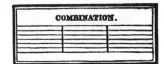

COMBINATION.

No. 372. 50 cts.   No. 373. 75 cts.

No. 374. 75 cts.   No. 376. 75 cts.

No. 375. 75 cts.

No. 377.　$3.

No. 378.　$1.50.

No. 379.　75 cts.

No. 381.　75 cts.

No. 380.　75 cts.

No. 382. $1.25.

No. 383.   62 cts.

No. 384.   18 cts.

No. 385. $1.

No. 386.   50 cts

No. 387.   25 cts.

Four lines Minion.

No. 388.   50 cts.

Four lines Brevier.

No. 389.   25 cts.

Four lines Brevier.

No. 390.   87 cts.

No. 391.   50 cts.

No. 392.   75 cts.

No. 393.   50 cts.

No. 394.   50 cts.　　　No. 395. $1.　　　No. 396.   50 cts.

No. 397.   25 cts.　　　　　　　No. 398.   25 cts.

No. 399.   75 cts.　　　　　No. 400.   75 cts.

No. 401. $1.25.

No. 402.   37 cts.

No. 403.   50 cts.

No. 404.   75 cts.

No. 405. $1.

No. 406.   37 cts.

No. 407. 37 cts.   No. 408. 37 cts.   No. 409. 37 cts.   No. 410.   37 cts.

No. 411. 18 cts.   No. 412. 18 cts.   No. 413. 18 cts.   No. 414. 18 cts.

No. 415.   25 cts.   No. 416. 10 cts.   No. 417. 10 cts.   No. 418. 10 cts.

No. 419. 10 cts.   No. 420. 10 cts.   No. 421. 10 cts.   No. 422. 10 cts.

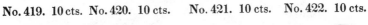 

141

No. 423. $1.50.

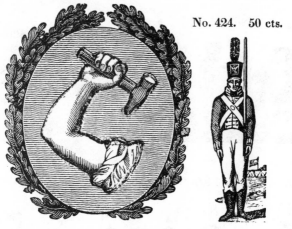

No. 424.   50 cts.

No. 425. $2.

No. 426. $2.

No. 427.　$2.50.

No. 428.　$1.50.

No. 429.　$1.

No. 430.　$1.

No. 431. $4.

No. 432 $ 1.50

FURNITURE

AND

No. 433: $ 1.25

No. 434. $ 1.

145

No. 435. $2.

No. 436. $1.50.

No. 437. $1.

146

No. 438. $1.

No. 439. $1.

No. 440. 50 cts.

No. 441. 37 cts.

No. 442.

10 cts.

8 cts.   6 cts.

No. 443. 12 cts.

No. 444. 10 cts.

No. 446. $1.

CROCKERY CHINA & GLASS WARES

No. 445. 37 cts.

No. 447. $1.25.

No. 448. $1.25.

No. 449. $1.25.

No. 451 $1.

No. 452. 87 cts.

No. 453. 87 cts.

No. 454. 75 cts.

No. 455. 75 cts.

No. 456. 75 cts.

No. 457. 37 cts.

No. 458. 25 cts.

No. 459. $1.75.

No. 460. $1.   No. 461.   37 cts.

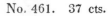

No. 462.   37 cts.

No. 463.   75 cts.   No. 464.   50 cts.

No. 465. $1.75.

No. 466. $1.50.

No. 467. $1.

No. 468.   50 cts.   No. 469.   50 cts.

No. 470.   25 cts.   No. 471.   25 cts.   No. 472.   25 cts.

No. 473. 37 cts.   No. 474.   37 cts.

No. 475.   37 cts.

No. 476.   37 cts.   No. 477.   50 cts.

No. 478.   37 cts.   No. 479.   25 cts.   No. 480.   25 cts.

153

No. 486. 1.25.

No. 483. 87 cts.

No. 485. $1.25.

No. 482. 75 cts

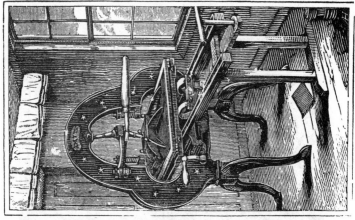

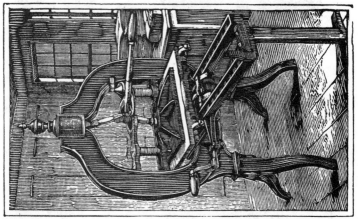

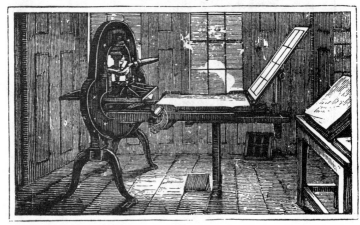

No. 490. $1.75.

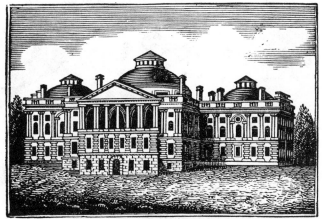

No. 491. $1.25.

No. 492. $1.25

No. 497.   12 cts.

No. 498.   25. cts.

No. 499.   37 cts.

No. 495. $1.25

No. 496. $1.

No. 493. $1.

No. 494. $1.

BOSTON TYPE AND STEREOTYPE FOUNDRY.

158

No. 500. **PRIMER CUTS,** 12 cts. single, or $8 per set.

159

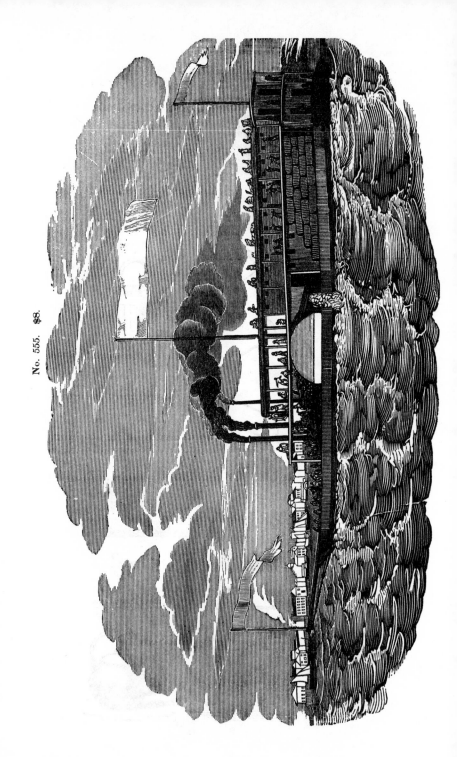

No. 502.   50 cts.

No. 503.   50 cts.

No. 504.   62 cts.

No. 505.   50 cts.

No. 507.   37 cts.

No. 506.   50 cts.

No. 508. 10 cts.   No. 509. 10 cts.   No. 510. 10 cts.

511. 10 cts.   512. 10 cts.   513. 12 cts.   514. 10 cts.

163

No. 517. 37 cts.

No. 520. 37 cts.

No. 515. $1.

No. 518. 50 cts.

No. 516. 75 cts.

No. 519. 75 cts.

No. 521. $1.

164

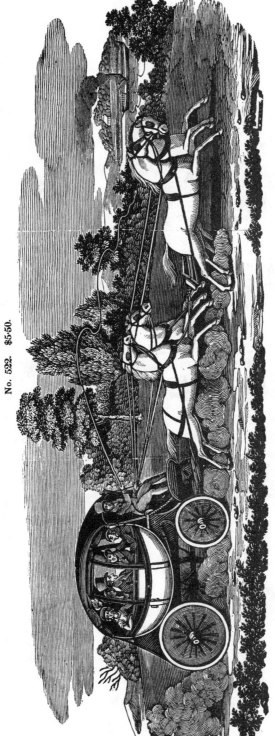

No. 522. $5·50.

No. 523. 62 cts.   No. 524. 25 cts.

No. 525. 18 cts.   No. 526. 37 cts.   No. 527. 12 cts.

No. 528. 37 cts.   No. 529. 37 cts.

No. 530. 37 cts.   No. 531. 37 cts.   No. 532.
                                            12 cts.

No. 533. 37 cts.

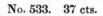

No. 534.   No. 535. 18 cts.
12 cts.

No. 536.   50 cts.   No. 537.   37 cts.

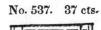

No. 538.   37 cts.

No. 540. 25 cts.   No. 541.   50 cts.

No. 542   25 cts.

No. 543.   50 cts.

No. 546.   50 cts.

No. 545.   37 cts.

167

No. 548. $2.00.

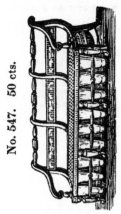

No. 547.   50 cts.

No. 549.   50 cts.

No. 550.   50 cts.

No. 552. $1.00.

No. 551.   50 cts.

No. 553.   50 cts.

No. 554. $3.00.

INDEPENDENCE.

No. 556.   50 cts.

No. 557.   62 cts.

No. 558.   37 cts.

No. 559.   50 cts.

No. 560.   50 cts.

No. 561.   50 cts.

No. 562.   37 cts.

No. 563.   50 cts.

No. 564.   62 cts.

No. 565. $1.25.

No. 566. $1.50.

No. 567. $1.25.

No. 568. 62 cts.

No. 569. 50 cts.

No. 570. 75 cts.

No. 571. 50 cts.

No. 572. 87 cts.

No. 573. 75 cts.

No. 574. 62½ cts.

No. 575. 82.

No. 576. 87 cts.

JEFFERSON.

No. 577. 50 cts.

No. 578. 62 cts.

No. 579. $1.25.

No. 580. $1.25.

No. 581. $1.

175

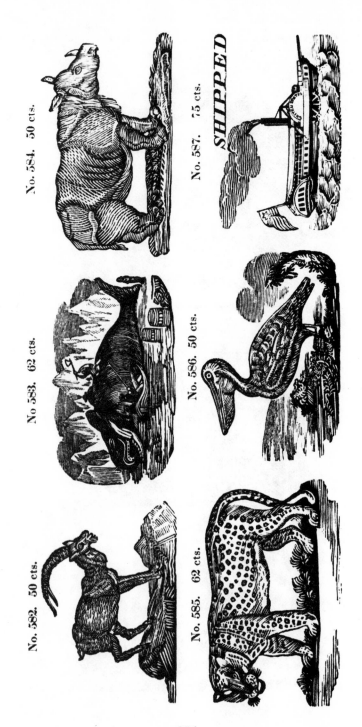

No. 584. 50 cts.

No. 587. 75 cts. *SHIPPED*

No 583. 62 cts.

No. 586. 50 cts.

No. 582. 50 cts.

No. 585. 62 cts.

No. 588. $1.

No. 589.   50 cts.

No. 590.   62 cts.

No. 591.   50 cts.

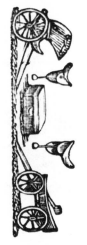

No. 592.   62 cts.

No. 593.   37 cts.

No. 594.   50 cts.

No. 596. $1.75.

No. 597. $1.75.

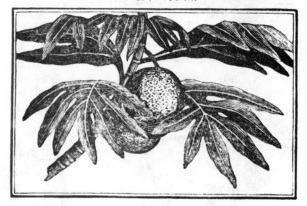

No. 598. $1.50.

No. 599. $1.25.

No. 600. $2.

No. 601. $1.50.

No. 602. $2.50.

No. 603.   75 cts.

No. 604. $1.25.

No. 605. $1.

No. 606. $1.

No. 607.   50 cts.

No. 608.   75 cts.

No. 609. $1.00.

No. 610.   50 cts.

No. 611.   62 cts.

No. 612.   50 cts.

No. 613.   25 cts.

No. 614.   25 cts.

No. 615.   10 cts.

No. 616.   10 cts.

WRITING

No 617.   50 cts.

No. 618.   75 cts

No. 619. $2.50.

No. 620. 75 cts.

No. 621. $1.00.

Bowen, sc.

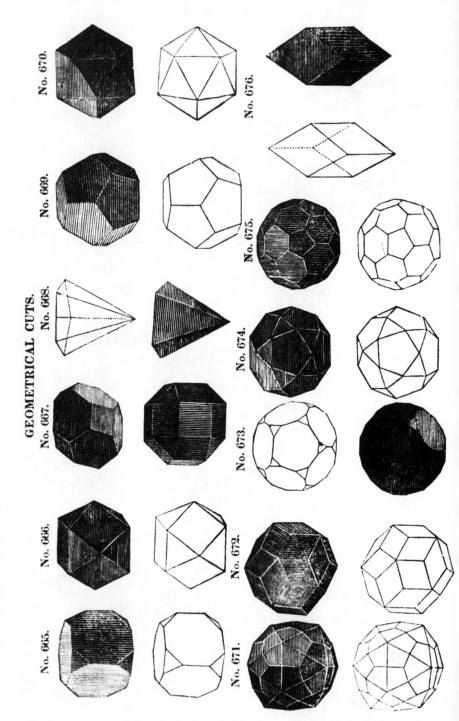

GEOMETRICAL CUTS.

No. 670.
No. 676.
No. 669.
No. 675.
No. 668.
No. 674.
No. 667.
No. 673.
No. 666.
No. 672.
No. 665.
No. 671.

A CATALOG OF SELECTED
DOVER BOOKS
IN ALL FIELDS OF INTEREST

A CATALOG OF SELECTED DOVER
BOOKS IN ALL FIELDS OF INTEREST

DRAWINGS OF REMBRANDT, edited by Seymour Slive. Updated Lippmann, Hofstede de Groot edition, with definitive scholarly apparatus. All portraits, biblical sketches, landscapes, nudes. Oriental figures, classical studies, together with selection of work by followers. 550 illustrations. Total of 630pp. 9⅛ × 12¼.
21485-0, 21486-9 Pa., Two-vol. set $25.00

GHOST AND HORROR STORIES OF AMBROSE BIERCE, Ambrose Bierce. 24 tales vividly imagined, strangely prophetic, and decades ahead of their time in technical skill: "The Damned Thing," "An Inhabitant of Carcosa," "The Eyes of the Panther," "Moxon's Master," and 20 more. 199pp. 5⅜ × 8½. 20767-6 Pa. $3.95

ETHICAL WRITINGS OF MAIMONIDES, Maimonides. Most significant ethical works of great medieval sage, newly translated for utmost precision, readability. Laws Concerning Character Traits, Eight Chapters, more. 192pp. 5⅜ × 8½.
24522-5 Pa. $4.50

THE EXPLORATION OF THE COLORADO RIVER AND ITS CANYONS, J. W. Powell. Full text of Powell's 1,000-mile expedition down the fabled Colorado in 1869. Superb account of terrain, geology, vegetation, Indians, famine, mutiny, treacherous rapids, mighty canyons, during exploration of last unknown part of continental U.S. 400pp. 5⅜ × 8½. 20094-9 Pa. $6.95

HISTORY OF PHILOSOPHY, Julián Marías. Clearest one-volume history on the market. Every major philosopher and dozens of others, to Existentialism and later. 505pp. 5⅜ × 8½. 21739-6 Pa. $8.50

ALL ABOUT LIGHTNING, Martin A. Uman. Highly readable non-technical survey of nature and causes of lightning, thunderstorms, ball lightning, St. Elmo's Fire, much more. Illustrated. 192pp. 5⅜ × 8½. 25237-X Pa. $5.95

SAILING ALONE AROUND THE WORLD, Captain Joshua Slocum. First man to sail around the world, alone, in small boat. One of great feats of seamanship told in delightful manner. 67 illustrations. 294pp. 5⅜ × 8½. 20326-3 Pa. $4.95

LETTERS AND NOTES ON THE MANNERS, CUSTOMS AND CONDITIONS OF THE NORTH AMERICAN INDIANS, George Catlin. Classic account of life among Plains Indians: ceremonies, hunt, warfare, etc. 312 plates. 572pp. of text. 6⅛ × 9¼. 22118-0, 22119-9 Pa. Two-vol. set $15.90

ALASKA: The Harriman Expedition, 1899, John Burroughs, John Muir, et al. Informative, engrossing accounts of two-month, 9,000-mile expedition. Native peoples, wildlife, forests, geography, salmon industry, glaciers, more. Profusely illustrated. 240 black-and-white line drawings. 124 black-and-white photographs. 3 maps. Index. 576pp. 5⅜ × 8½. 25109-8 Pa. $11.95

THE BOOK OF BEASTS: Being a Translation from a Latin Bestiary of the Twelfth Century, T. H. White. Wonderful catalog real and fanciful beasts: manticore, griffin, phoenix, amphivius, jaculus, many more. White's witty erudite commentary on scientific, historical aspects. Fascinating glimpse of medieval mind. Illustrated. 296pp. 5⅜ × 8¼. (Available in U.S. only) 24609-4 Pa. $5.95

FRANK LLOYD WRIGHT: ARCHITECTURE AND NATURE With 160 Illustrations, Donald Hoffmann. Profusely illustrated study of influence of nature—especially prairie—on Wright's designs for Fallingwater, Robie House, Guggenheim Museum, other masterpieces. 96pp. 9¼ × 10¾. 25098-9 Pa. $7.95

FRANK LLOYD WRIGHT'S FALLINGWATER, Donald Hoffmann. Wright's famous waterfall house: planning and construction of organic idea. History of site, owners, Wright's personal involvement. Photographs of various stages of building. Preface by Edgar Kaufmann, Jr. 100 illustrations. 112pp. 9¼ × 10. 23671-4 Pa. $7.95

YEARS WITH FRANK LLOYD WRIGHT: Apprentice to Genius, Edgar Tafel. Insightful memoir by a former apprentice presents a revealing portrait of Wright the man, the inspired teacher, the greatest American architect. 372 black-and-white illustrations. Preface. Index. vi + 228pp. 8¼ × 11. 24801-1 Pa. $9.95

THE STORY OF KING ARTHUR AND HIS KNIGHTS, Howard Pyle. Enchanting version of King Arthur fable has delighted generations with imaginative narratives of exciting adventures and unforgettable illustrations by the author. 41 illustrations. xviii + 313pp. 6⅛ × 9¼. 21445-1 Pa. $6.50

THE GODS OF THE EGYPTIANS, E. A. Wallis Budge. Thorough coverage of numerous gods of ancient Egypt by foremost Egyptologist. Information on evolution of cults, rites and gods; the cult of Osiris; the Book of the Dead and its rites; the sacred animals and birds; Heaven and Hell; and more. 956pp. 6⅛ × 9¼. 22055-9, 22056-7 Pa., Two-vol. set $20.00

A THEOLOGICO-POLITICAL TREATISE, Benedict Spinoza. Also contains unfinished Political Treatise. Great classic on religious liberty, theory of government on common consent. R. Elwes translation. Total of 421pp. 5⅜ × 8½. 20249-6 Pa. $6.95

INCIDENTS OF TRAVEL IN CENTRAL AMERICA, CHIAPAS, AND YUCATAN, John L. Stephens. Almost single-handed discovery of Maya culture; exploration of ruined cities, monuments, temples; customs of Indians. 115 drawings. 892pp. 5⅜ × 8½. 22404-X, 22405-8 Pa., Two-vol. set $15.90

LOS CAPRICHOS, Francisco Goya. 80 plates of wild, grotesque monsters and caricatures. Prado manuscript included. 183pp. 6⅜ × 9⅜. 22384-1 Pa. $4.95

AUTOBIOGRAPHY: The Story of My Experiments with Truth, Mohandas K. Gandhi. Not hagiography, but Gandhi in his own words. Boyhood, legal studies, purification, the growth of the Satyagraha (nonviolent protest) movement. Critical, inspiring work of the man who freed India. 480pp. 5⅜ × 8½. (Available in U.S. only) 24593-4 Pa. $6.95

ILLUSTRATED DICTIONARY OF HISTORIC ARCHITECTURE, edited by Cyril M. Harris. Extraordinary compendium of clear, concise definitions for over 5,000 important architectural terms complemented by over 2,000 line drawings. Covers full spectrum of architecture from ancient ruins to 20th-century Modernism. Preface. 592pp. 7½ × 9⅝. 24444-X Pa. $14.95

THE NIGHT BEFORE CHRISTMAS, Clement Moore. Full text, and woodcuts from original 1848 book. Also critical, historical material. 19 illustrations. 40pp. 4⅝ × 6. 22797-9 Pa. $2.25

THE LESSON OF JAPANESE ARCHITECTURE: 165 Photographs, Jiro Harada. Memorable gallery of 165 photographs taken in the 1930's of exquisite Japanese homes of the well-to-do and historic buildings. 13 line diagrams. 192pp. 8⅜ × 11¼. 24778-3 Pa. $8.95

THE AUTOBIOGRAPHY OF CHARLES DARWIN AND SELECTED LETTERS, edited by Francis Darwin. The fascinating life of eccentric genius composed of an intimate memoir by Darwin (intended for his children); commentary by his son, Francis; hundreds of fragments from notebooks, journals, papers; and letters to and from Lyell, Hooker, Huxley, Wallace and Henslow. xi + 365pp. 5⅜ × 8. 20479-0 Pa. $6.95

WONDERS OF THE SKY: Observing Rainbows, Comets, Eclipses, the Stars and Other Phenomena, Fred Schaaf. Charming, easy-to-read poetic guide to all manner of celestial events visible to the naked eye. Mock suns, glories, Belt of Venus, more. Illustrated. 299pp. 5¼ × 8¼. 24402-4 Pa. $7.95

BURNHAM'S CELESTIAL HANDBOOK, Robert Burnham, Jr. Thorough guide to the stars beyond our solar system. Exhaustive treatment. Alphabetical by constellation: Andromeda to Cetus in Vol. 1; Chamaeleon to Orion in Vol. 2; and Pavo to Vulpecula in Vol. 3. Hundreds of illustrations. Index in Vol. 3. 2,000pp. 6⅛ × 9¼. 23567-X, 23568-8, 23673-0 Pa., Three-vol. set $38.85

STAR NAMES: Their Lore and Meaning, Richard Hinckley Allen. Fascinating history of names various cultures have given to constellations and literary and folkloristic uses that have been made of stars. Indexes to subjects. Arabic and Greek names. Biblical references. Bibliography. 563pp. 5⅜ × 8½. 21079-0 Pa. $7.95

THIRTY YEARS THAT SHOOK PHYSICS: The Story of Quantum Theory, George Gamow. Lucid, accessible introduction to influential theory of energy and matter. Careful explanations of Dirac's anti-particles, Bohr's model of the atom, much more. 12 plates. Numerous drawings. 240pp. 5⅜ × 8½. 24895-X Pa. $4.95

CHINESE DOMESTIC FURNITURE IN PHOTOGRAPHS AND MEASURED DRAWINGS, Gustav Ecke. A rare volume, now affordably priced for antique collectors, furniture buffs and art historians. Detailed review of styles ranging from early Shang to late Ming. Unabridged republication. 161 black-and-white drawings, photos. Total of 224pp. 8⅜ × 11¼. (Available in U.S. only) 25171-3 Pa. $12.95

VINCENT VAN GOGH: A Biography, Julius Meier-Graefe. Dynamic, penetrating study of artist's life, relationship with brother, Theo, painting techniques, travels, more. Readable, engrossing. 160pp. 5⅜ × 8½. (Available in U.S. only) 25253-1 Pa. $3.95

HOW TO WRITE, Gertrude Stein. Gertrude Stein claimed anyone could understand her unconventional writing—here are clues to help. Fascinating improvisations, language experiments, explanations illuminate Stein's craft and the art of writing. Total of 414pp. 4⅜ × 6⅜. 23144-5 Pa. $5.95

ADVENTURES AT SEA IN THE GREAT AGE OF SAIL: Five Firsthand Narratives, edited by Elliot Snow. Rare true accounts of exploration, whaling, shipwreck, fierce natives, trade, shipboard life, more. 33 illustrations. Introduction. 353pp. 5⅜ × 8½. 25177-2 Pa. $7.95

THE HERBAL OR GENERAL HISTORY OF PLANTS, John Gerard. Classic descriptions of about 2,850 plants—with over 2,700 illustrations—includes Latin and English names, physical descriptions, varieties, time and place of growth, more. 2,706 illustrations. xlv + 1,678pp. 8½ × 12¼. 23147-X Cloth. $75.00

DOROTHY AND THE WIZARD IN OZ, L. Frank Baum. Dorothy and the Wizard visit the center of the Earth, where people are vegetables, glass houses grow and Oz characters reappear. Classic sequel to *Wizard of Oz*. 256pp. 5⅜ × 8. 24714-7 Pa. $4.95

SONGS OF EXPERIENCE: Facsimile Reproduction with 26 Plates in Full Color, William Blake. This facsimile of Blake's original "Illuminated Book" reproduces 26 full-color plates from a rare 1826 edition. Includes "The Tyger," "London," "Holy Thursday," and other immortal poems. 26 color plates. Printed text of poems. 48pp. 5¼ × 7. 24636-1 Pa. $3.50

SONGS OF INNOCENCE, William Blake. The first and most popular of Blake's famous "Illuminated Books," in a facsimile edition reproducing all 31 brightly colored plates. Additional printed text of each poem. 64pp. 5¼ × 7. 22764-2 Pa. $3.50

PRECIOUS STONES, Max Bauer. Classic, thorough study of diamonds, rubies, emeralds, garnets, etc.: physical character, occurrence, properties, use, similar topics. 20 plates, 8 in color. 94 figures. 659pp. 6⅛ × 9¼. 21910-0, 21911-9 Pa., Two-vol. set $15.90

ENCYCLOPEDIA OF VICTORIAN NEEDLEWORK, S. F. A. Caulfeild and Blanche Saward. Full, precise descriptions of stitches, techniques for dozens of needlecrafts—most exhaustive reference of its kind. Over 800 figures. Total of 679pp. 8⅛ × 11. Two volumes. Vol. 1 22800-2 Pa. $11.95
Vol. 2 22801-0 Pa. $11.95

THE MARVELOUS LAND OF OZ, L. Frank Baum. Second Oz book, the Scarecrow and Tin Woodman are back with hero named Tip, Oz magic. 136 illustrations. 287pp. 5⅜ × 8½. 20692-0 Pa. $5.95

WILD FOWL DECOYS, Joel Barber. Basic book on the subject, by foremost authority and collector. Reveals history of decoy making and rigging, place in American culture, different kinds of decoys, how to make them, and how to use them. 140 plates. 156pp. 7⅞ × 10¾. 20011-6 Pa. $8.95

HISTORY OF LACE, Mrs. Bury Palliser. Definitive, profusely illustrated chronicle of lace from earliest times to late 19th century. Laces of Italy, Greece, England, France, Belgium, etc. Landmark of needlework scholarship. 266 illustrations. 672pp. 6⅛ × 9¼. 24742-2 Pa. $14.95

ILLUSTRATED GUIDE TO SHAKER FURNITURE, Robert Meader. All furniture and appurtenances, with much on unknown local styles. 235 photos. 146pp. 9 × 12. 22819-3 Pa. $7.95

WHALE SHIPS AND WHALING: A Pictorial Survey, George Francis Dow. Over 200 vintage engravings, drawings, photographs of barks, brigs, cutters, other vessels. Also harpoons, lances, whaling guns, many other artifacts. Comprehensive text by foremost authority. 207 black-and-white illustrations. 288pp. 6 × 9. 24808-9 Pa. $8.95

THE BERTRAMS, Anthony Trollope. Powerful portrayal of blind self-will and thwarted ambition includes one of Trollope's most heartrending love stories. 497pp. 5⅜ × 8½. 25119-5 Pa. $8.95

ADVENTURES WITH A HAND LENS, Richard Headstrom. Clearly written guide to observing and studying flowers and grasses, fish scales, moth and insect wings, egg cases, buds, feathers, seeds, leaf scars, moss, molds, ferns, common crystals, etc.—all with an ordinary, inexpensive magnifying glass. 209 exact line drawings aid in your discoveries. 220pp. 5⅜ × 8½. 23330-8 Pa. $3.95

RODIN ON ART AND ARTISTS, Auguste Rodin. Great sculptor's candid, wide-ranging comments on meaning of art; great artists; relation of sculpture to poetry, painting, music; philosophy of life, more. 76 superb black-and-white illustrations of Rodin's sculpture, drawings and prints. 119pp. 8⅜ × 11¼. 24487-3 Pa. $6.95

FIFTY CLASSIC FRENCH FILMS, 1912–1982: A Pictorial Record, Anthony Slide. Memorable stills from Grand Illusion, Beauty and the Beast, Hiroshima, Mon Amour, many more. Credits, plot synopses, reviews, etc. 160pp. 8¼ × 11. 25256-6 Pa. $11.95

THE PRINCIPLES OF PSYCHOLOGY, William James. Famous long course complete, unabridged. Stream of thought, time perception, memory, experimental methods; great work decades ahead of its time. 94 figures. 1,391pp. 5⅜ × 8½. 20381-6, 20382-4 Pa., Two-vol. set $19.90

BODIES IN A BOOKSHOP, R. T. Campbell. Challenging mystery of blackmail and murder with ingenious plot and superbly drawn characters. In the best tradition of British suspense fiction. 192pp. 5⅜ × 8½. 24720-1 Pa. $3.95

CALLAS: PORTRAIT OF A PRIMA DONNA, George Jellinek. Renowned commentator on the musical scene chronicles incredible career and life of the most controversial, fascinating, influential operatic personality of our time. 64 black-and-white photographs. 416pp. 5⅜ × 8¼. 25047-4 Pa. $7.95

GEOMETRY, RELATIVITY AND THE FOURTH DIMENSION, Rudolph Rucker. Exposition of fourth dimension, concepts of relativity as Flatland characters continue adventures. Popular, easily followed yet accurate, profound. 141 illustrations. 133pp. 5⅜ × 8½. 23400-2 Pa. $3.95

HOUSEHOLD STORIES BY THE BROTHERS GRIMM, with pictures by Walter Crane. 53 classic stories—Rumpelstiltskin, Rapunzel, Hansel and Gretel, the Fisherman and his Wife, Snow White, Tom Thumb, Sleeping Beauty, Cinderella, and so much more—lavishly illustrated with original 19th century drawings. 114 illustrations. x + 269pp. 5⅜ × 8½. 21080-4 Pa. $4.50

SUNDIALS, Albert Waugh. Far and away the best, most thorough coverage of ideas, mathematics concerned, types, construction, adjusting anywhere. Over 100 illustrations. 230pp. 5⅜ × 8½. 22947-5 Pa. $4.50

PICTURE HISTORY OF THE NORMANDIE: With 190 Illustrations, Frank O. Braynard. Full story of legendary French ocean liner: Art Deco interiors, design innovations, furnishings, celebrities, maiden voyage, tragic fire, much more. Extensive text. 144pp. 8⅞ × 11¾. 25257-4 Pa. $9.95

THE FIRST AMERICAN COOKBOOK: A Facsimile of "American Cookery," 1796, Amelia Simmons. Facsimile of the first American-written cookbook published in the United States contains authentic recipes for colonial favorites—pumpkin pudding, winter squash pudding, spruce beer, Indian slapjacks, and more. Introductory Essay and Glossary of colonial cooking terms. 80pp. 5⅜ × 8½. 24710-4 Pa. $3.50

101 PUZZLES IN THOUGHT AND LOGIC, C. R. Wylie, Jr. Solve murders and robberies, find out which fishermen are liars, how a blind man could possibly identify a color—purely by your own reasoning! 107pp. 5⅜ × 8½. 20367-0 Pa. $2.50

THE BOOK OF WORLD-FAMOUS MUSIC—CLASSICAL, POPULAR AND FOLK, James J. Fuld. Revised and enlarged republication of landmark work in musico-bibliography. Full information about nearly 1,000 songs and compositions including first lines of music and lyrics. New supplement. Index. 800pp. 5⅜ × 8¼. 24857-7 Pa. $14.95

ANTHROPOLOGY AND MODERN LIFE, Franz Boas. Great anthropologist's classic treatise on race and culture. Introduction by Ruth Bunzel. Only inexpensive paperback edition. 255pp. 5⅜ × 8½. 25245-0 Pa. $5.95

THE TALE OF PETER RABBIT, Beatrix Potter. The inimitable Peter's terrifying adventure in Mr. McGregor's garden, with all 27 wonderful, full-color Potter illustrations. 55pp. 4¼ × 5½. (Available in U.S. only) 22827-4 Pa. $1.75

THREE PROPHETIC SCIENCE FICTION NOVELS, H. G. Wells. *When the Sleeper Wakes, A Story of the Days to Come* and *The Time Machine* (full version). 335pp. 5⅜ × 8½. (Available in U.S. only) 20605-X Pa. $5.95

APICIUS COOKERY AND DINING IN IMPERIAL ROME, edited and translated by Joseph Dommers Vehling. Oldest known cookbook in existence offers readers a clear picture of what foods Romans ate, how they prepared them, etc. 49 illustrations. 301pp. 6⅛ × 9¼. 23563-7 Pa. $6.50

SHAKESPEARE LEXICON AND QUOTATION DICTIONARY, Alexander Schmidt. Full definitions, locations, shades of meaning of every word in plays and poems. More than 50,000 exact quotations. 1,485pp. 6½ × 9¼. 22726-X, 22727-8 Pa., Two-vol. set $27.90

THE WORLD'S GREAT SPEECHES, edited by Lewis Copeland and Lawrence W. Lamm. Vast collection of 278 speeches from Greeks to 1970. Powerful and effective models; unique look at history. 842pp. 5⅜ × 8½. 20468-5 Pa. $11.95

THE BLUE FAIRY BOOK, Andrew Lang. The first, most famous collection, with many familiar tales: Little Red Riding Hood, Aladdin and the Wonderful Lamp, Puss in Boots, Sleeping Beauty, Hansel and Gretel, Rumpelstiltskin; 37 in all. 138 illustrations. 390pp. 5⅜ × 8½. 21437-0 Pa. $5.95

THE STORY OF THE CHAMPIONS OF THE ROUND TABLE, Howard Pyle. Sir Launcelot, Sir Tristram and Sir Percival in spirited adventures of love and triumph retold in Pyle's inimitable style. 50 drawings, 31 full-page. xviii + 329pp. 6½ × 9¼. 21883-X Pa. $6.95

AUDUBON AND HIS JOURNALS, Maria Audubon. Unmatched two-volume portrait of the great artist, naturalist and author contains his journals, an excellent biography by his granddaughter, expert annotations by the noted ornithologist, Dr. Elliott Coues, and 37 superb illustrations. Total of 1,200pp. 5⅜ × 8.
Vol. I 25143-8 Pa. $8.95
Vol. II 25144-6 Pa. $8.95

GREAT DINOSAUR HUNTERS AND THEIR DISCOVERIES, Edwin H. Colbert. Fascinating, lavishly illustrated chronicle of dinosaur research, 1820's to 1960. Achievements of Cope, Marsh, Brown, Buckland, Mantell, Huxley, many others. 384pp. 5¼ × 8¼. 24701-5 Pa. $6.95

THE TASTEMAKERS, Russell Lynes. Informal, illustrated social history of American taste 1850's–1950's. First popularized categories Highbrow, Lowbrow, Middlebrow. 129 illustrations. New (1979) afterword. 384pp. 6 × 9.
23993-4 Pa. $6.95

DOUBLE CROSS PURPOSES, Ronald A. Knox. A treasure hunt in the Scottish Highlands, an old map, unidentified corpse, surprise discoveries keep reader guessing in this cleverly intricate tale of financial skullduggery. 2 black-and-white maps. 320pp. 5⅜ × 8½. (Available in U.S. only) 25032-6 Pa. $5.95

AUTHENTIC VICTORIAN DECORATION AND ORNAMENTATION IN FULL COLOR: 46 Plates from "Studies in Design," Christopher Dresser. Superb full-color lithographs reproduced from rare original portfolio of a major Victorian designer. 48pp. 9¼ × 12¼. 25083-0 Pa. $7.95

PRIMITIVE ART, Franz Boas. Remains the best text ever prepared on subject, thoroughly discussing Indian, African, Asian, Australian, and, especially, Northern American primitive art. Over 950 illustrations show ceramics, masks, totem poles, weapons, textiles, paintings, much more. 376pp. 5⅜ × 8. 20025-6 Pa. $6.95

SIDELIGHTS ON RELATIVITY, Albert Einstein. Unabridged republication of two lectures delivered by the great physicist in 1920–21. *Ether and Relativity* and *Geometry and Experience*. Elegant ideas in non-mathematical form, accessible to intelligent layman. vi + 56pp. 5⅜ × 8½. 24511-X Pa. $2.95

THE WIT AND HUMOR OF OSCAR WILDE, edited by Alvin Redman. More than 1,000 ripostes, paradoxes, wisecracks: Work is the curse of the drinking classes, I can resist everything except temptation, etc. 258pp. 5⅜ × 8½. 20602-5 Pa. $4.50

ADVENTURES WITH A MICROSCOPE, Richard Headstrom. 59 adventures with clothing fibers, protozoa, ferns and lichens, roots and leaves, much more. 142 illustrations. 232pp. 5⅜ × 8½. 23471-1 Pa. $3.95

PLANTS OF THE BIBLE, Harold N. Moldenke and Alma L. Moldenke. Standard reference to all 230 plants mentioned in Scriptures. Latin name, biblical reference, uses, modern identity, much more. Unsurpassed encyclopedic resource for scholars, botanists, nature lovers, students of Bible. Bibliography. Indexes. 123 black-and-white illustrations. 384pp. 6 × 9. 25069-5 Pa. $8.95

FAMOUS AMERICAN WOMEN: A Biographical Dictionary from Colonial Times to the Present, Robert McHenry, ed. From Pocahontas to Rosa Parks, 1,035 distinguished American women documented in separate biographical entries. Accurate, up-to-date data, numerous categories, spans 400 years. Indices. 493pp. 6½ × 9¼. 24523-3 Pa. $9.95

THE FABULOUS INTERIORS OF THE GREAT OCEAN LINERS IN HISTORIC PHOTOGRAPHS, William H. Miller, Jr. Some 200 superb photographs capture exquisite interiors of world's great "floating palaces"—1890's to 1980's: *Titanic, Ile de France, Queen Elizabeth, United States, Europa,* more. Approx. 200 black-and-white photographs. Captions. Text. Introduction. 160pp. 8⅞ × 11¾. 24756-2 Pa. $9.95

THE GREAT LUXURY LINERS, 1927–1954: A Photographic Record, William H. Miller, Jr. Nostalgic tribute to heyday of ocean liners. 186 photos of Ile de France, Normandie, Leviathan, Queen Elizabeth, United States, many others. Interior and exterior views. Introduction. Captions. 160pp. 9 × 12. 24056-8 Pa. $9.95

A NATURAL HISTORY OF THE DUCKS, John Charles Phillips. Great landmark of ornithology offers complete detailed coverage of nearly 200 species and subspecies of ducks: gadwall, sheldrake, merganser, pintail, many more. 74 full-color plates, 102 black-and-white. Bibliography. Total of 1,920pp. 8⅝ × 11¼. 25141-1, 25142-X Cloth. Two-vol. set $100.00

THE SEAWEED HANDBOOK: An Illustrated Guide to Seaweeds from North Carolina to Canada, Thomas F. Lee. Concise reference covers 78 species. Scientific and common names, habitat, distribution, more. Finding keys for easy identification. 224pp. 5⅜ × 8½. 25215-9 Pa. $5.95

THE TEN BOOKS OF ARCHITECTURE: The 1755 Leoni Edition, Leon Battista Alberti. Rare classic helped introduce the glories of ancient architecture to the Renaissance. 68 black-and-white plates. 336pp. 8⅜ × 11¼. 25239-6 Pa. $14.95

MISS MACKENZIE, Anthony Trollope. Minor masterpieces by Victorian master unmasks many truths about life in 19th-century England. First inexpensive edition in years. 392pp. 5⅜ × 8½. 25201-9 Pa. $7.95

THE RIME OF THE ANCIENT MARINER, Gustave Doré, Samuel Taylor Coleridge. Dramatic engravings considered by many to be his greatest work. The terrifying space of the open sea, the storms and whirlpools of an unknown ocean, the ice of Antarctica, more—all rendered in a powerful, chilling manner. Full text. 38 plates. 77pp. 9¼ × 12. 22305-1 Pa. $4.95

THE EXPEDITIONS OF ZEBULON MONTGOMERY PIKE, Zebulon Montgomery Pike. Fascinating first-hand accounts (1805–6) of exploration of Mississippi River, Indian wars, capture by Spanish dragoons, much more. 1,088pp. 5⅜ × 8½. 25254-X, 25255-8 Pa. Two-vol. set $23.90

A CONCISE HISTORY OF PHOTOGRAPHY: Third Revised Edition, Helmut Gernsheim. Best one-volume history—camera obscura, photochemistry, daguerreotypes, evolution of cameras, film, more. Also artistic aspects—landscape, portraits, fine art, etc. 281 black-and-white photographs. 26 in color. 176pp. 8⅜ × 11¼. 25128-4 Pa. $12.95

THE DORÉ BIBLE ILLUSTRATIONS, Gustave Doré. 241 detailed plates from the Bible: the Creation scenes, Adam and Eve, Flood, Babylon, battle sequences, life of Jesus, etc. Each plate is accompanied by the verses from the King James version of the Bible. 241pp. 9 × 12. 23004-X Pa. $8.95

HUGGER-MUGGER IN THE LOUVRE, Elliot Paul. Second Homer Evans mystery-comedy. Theft at the Louvre involves sleuth in hilarious, madcap caper. "A knockout."—Books. 336pp. 5⅜ × 8½. 25185-3 Pa. $5.95

FLATLAND, E. A. Abbott. Intriguing and enormously popular science-fiction classic explores the complexities of trying to survive as a two-dimensional being in a three-dimensional world. Amusingly illustrated by the author. 16 illustrations. 103pp. 5⅜ × 8½. 20001-9 Pa. $2.25

THE HISTORY OF THE LEWIS AND CLARK EXPEDITION, Meriwether Lewis and William Clark, edited by Elliott Coues. Classic edition of Lewis and Clark's day-by-day journals that later became the basis for U.S. claims to Oregon and the West. Accurate and invaluable geographical, botanical, biological, meteorological and anthropological material. Total of 1,508pp. 5⅜ × 8½.
21268-8, 21269-6, 21270-X Pa. Three-vol. set $25.50

LANGUAGE, TRUTH AND LOGIC, Alfred J. Ayer. Famous, clear introduction to Vienna, Cambridge schools of Logical Positivism. Role of philosophy, elimination of metaphysics, nature of analysis, etc. 160pp. 5⅜ × 8½. (Available in U.S. and Canada only) 20010-8 Pa. $2.95

MATHEMATICS FOR THE NONMATHEMATICIAN, Morris Kline. Detailed, college-level treatment of mathematics in cultural and historical context, with numerous exercises. For liberal arts students. Preface. Recommended Reading Lists. Tables. Index. Numerous black-and-white figures. xvi + 641pp. 5⅜ × 8½.
24823-2 Pa. $11.95

28 SCIENCE FICTION STORIES, H. G. Wells. Novels, *Star Begotten* and *Men Like Gods*, plus 26 short stories: "Empire of the Ants," "A Story of the Stone Age," "The Stolen Bacillus," "In the Abyss," etc. 915pp. 5⅜ × 8½. (Available in U.S. only)
20265-8 Cloth. $10.95

HANDBOOK OF PICTORIAL SYMBOLS, Rudolph Modley. 3,250 signs and symbols, many systems in full; official or heavy commercial use. Arranged by subject. Most in Pictorial Archive series. 143pp. 8⅜ × 11. 23357-X Pa. $5.95

INCIDENTS OF TRAVEL IN YUCATAN, John L. Stephens. Classic (1843) exploration of jungles of Yucatan, looking for evidences of Maya civilization. Travel adventures, Mexican and Indian culture, etc. Total of 669pp. 5⅜ × 8½.
20926-1, 20927-X Pa., Two-vol. set $9.90

DEGAS: An Intimate Portrait, Ambroise Vollard. Charming, anecdotal memoir by famous art dealer of one of the greatest 19th-century French painters. 14 black-and-white illustrations. Introduction by Harold L. Van Doren. 96pp. 5⅜ × 8½.
25131-4 Pa. $3.95

PERSONAL NARRATIVE OF A PILGRIMAGE TO ALMANDINAH AND MECCAH, Richard Burton. Great travel classic by remarkably colorful personality. Burton, disguised as a Moroccan, visited sacred shrines of Islam, narrowly escaping death. 47 illustrations. 959pp. 5⅜ × 8½. 21217-3, 21218-1 Pa., Two-vol. set $19.90

PHRASE AND WORD ORIGINS, A. H. Holt. Entertaining, reliable, modern study of more than 1,200 colorful words, phrases, origins and histories. Much unexpected information. 254pp. 5⅜ × 8½. 20758-7 Pa. $4.95

THE RED THUMB MARK, R. Austin Freeman. In this first Dr. Thorndyke case, the great scientific detective draws fascinating conclusions from the nature of a single fingerprint. Exciting story, authentic science. 320pp. 5⅜ × 8½. (Available in U.S. only) 25210-8 Pa. $5.95

AN EGYPTIAN HIEROGLYPHIC DICTIONARY, E. A. Wallis Budge. Monumental work containing about 25,000 words or terms that occur in texts ranging from 3000 B.C. to 600 A.D. Each entry consists of a transliteration of the word, the word in hieroglyphs, and the meaning in English. 1,314pp. 6⅜ × 10.
23615-3, 23616-1 Pa., Two-vol. set $27.90

THE COMPLEAT STRATEGYST: Being a Primer on the Theory of Games of Strategy, J. D. Williams. Highly entertaining classic describes, with many illustrated examples, how to select best strategies in conflict situations. Prefaces. Appendices. xvi + 268pp. 5⅜ × 8½. 25101-2 Pa. $5.95

THE ROAD TO OZ, L. Frank Baum. Dorothy meets the Shaggy Man, little Button-Bright and the Rainbow's beautiful daughter in this delightful trip to the magical Land of Oz. 272pp. 5⅜ × 8. 25208-6 Pa. $4.95

POINT AND LINE TO PLANE, Wassily Kandinsky. Seminal exposition of role of point, line, other elements in non-objective painting. Essential to understanding 20th-century art. 127 illustrations. 192pp. 6½ × 9¼. 23808-3 Pa. $4.50

LADY ANNA, Anthony Trollope. Moving chronicle of Countess Lovel's bitter struggle to win for herself and daughter Anna their rightful rank and fortune— perhaps at cost of sanity itself. 384pp. 5⅜ × 8½. 24669-8 Pa. $6.95

EGYPTIAN MAGIC, E. A. Wallis Budge. Sums up all that is known about magic in Ancient Egypt: the role of magic in controlling the gods, powerful amulets that warded off evil spirits, scarabs of immortality, use of wax images, formulas and spells, the secret name, much more. 253pp. 5⅜ × 8½. 22681-6 Pa. $4.00

THE DANCE OF SIVA, Ananda Coomaraswamy. Preeminent authority unfolds the vast metaphysic of India: the revelation of her art, conception of the universe, social organization, etc. 27 reproductions of art masterpieces. 192pp. 5⅜ × 8½.
24817-8 Pa. $5.95

CHRISTMAS CUSTOMS AND TRADITIONS, Clement A. Miles. Origin, evolution, significance of religious, secular practices. Caroling, gifts, yule logs, much more. Full, scholarly yet fascinating; non-sectarian. 400pp. 5⅜ × 8½.
23354-5 Pa. $6.50

THE HUMAN FIGURE IN MOTION, Eadweard Muybridge. More than 4,500 stopped-action photos, in action series, showing undraped men, women, children jumping, lying down, throwing, sitting, wrestling, carrying, etc. 390pp. 7⅞ × 10⅝.
20204-6 Cloth. $21.95

THE MAN WHO WAS THURSDAY, Gilbert Keith Chesterton. Witty, fast-paced novel about a club of anarchists in turn-of-the-century London. Brilliant social, religious, philosophical speculations. 128pp. 5⅜ × 8½.
25121-7 Pa. $3.95

A CEZANNE SKETCHBOOK: Figures, Portraits, Landscapes and Still Lifes, Paul Cezanne. Great artist experiments with tonal effects, light, mass, other qualities in over 100 drawings. A revealing view of developing master painter, precursor of Cubism. 102 black-and-white illustrations. 144pp. 8¾ × 6⅝.
24790-2 Pa. $5.95

AN ENCYCLOPEDIA OF BATTLES: Accounts of Over 1,560 Battles from 1479 B.C. to the Present, David Eggenberger. Presents essential details of every major battle in recorded history, from the first battle of Megiddo in 1479 B.C. to Grenada in 1984. List of Battle Maps. New Appendix covering the years 1967–1984. Index. 99 illustrations. 544pp. 6½ × 9¼.
24913-1 Pa. $14.95

AN ETYMOLOGICAL DICTIONARY OF MODERN ENGLISH, Ernest Weekley. Richest, fullest work, by foremost British lexicographer. Detailed word histories. Inexhaustible. Total of 856pp. 6½ × 9¼.
21873-2, 21874-0 Pa., Two-vol. set $17.00

WEBSTER'S AMERICAN MILITARY BIOGRAPHIES, edited by Robert McHenry. Over 1,000 figures who shaped 3 centuries of American military history. Detailed biographies of Nathan Hale, Douglas MacArthur, Mary Hallaren, others. Chronologies of engagements, more. Introduction. Addenda. 1,033 entries in alphabetical order. xi + 548pp. 6½ × 9¼. (Available in U.S. only)
24758-9 Pa. $11.95

LIFE IN ANCIENT EGYPT, Adolf Erman. Detailed older account, with much not in more recent books: domestic life, religion, magic, medicine, commerce, and whatever else needed for complete picture. Many illustrations. 597pp. 5⅜ × 8½.
22632-8 Pa. $8.50

HISTORIC COSTUME IN PICTURES, Braun & Schneider. Over 1,450 costumed figures shown, covering a wide variety of peoples: kings, emperors, nobles, priests, servants, soldiers, scholars, townsfolk, peasants, merchants, courtiers, cavaliers, and more. 256pp. 8⅜ × 11¼.
23150-X Pa. $7.95

THE NOTEBOOKS OF LEONARDO DA VINCI, edited by J. P. Richter. Extracts from manuscripts reveal great genius; on painting, sculpture, anatomy, sciences, geography, etc. Both Italian and English. 186 ms. pages reproduced, plus 500 additional drawings, including studies for *Last Supper, Sforza* monument, etc. 860pp. 7⅞ × 10¾. (Available in U.S. only) 22572-0, 22573-9 Pa., Two-vol. set $25.90

THE ART NOUVEAU STYLE BOOK OF ALPHONSE MUCHA: All 72 Plates from "Documents Decoratifs" in Original Color, Alphonse Mucha. Rare copyright-free design portfolio by high priest of Art Nouveau. Jewelry, wallpaper, stained glass, furniture, figure studies, plant and animal motifs, etc. Only complete one-volume edition. 80pp. 9⅜ × 12¼.   24044-4 Pa. $8.95

ANIMALS: 1,419 COPYRIGHT-FREE ILLUSTRATIONS OF MAMMALS, BIRDS, FISH, INSECTS, ETC., edited by Jim Harter. Clear wood engravings present, in extremely lifelike poses, over 1,000 species of animals. One of the most extensive pictorial sourcebooks of its kind. Captions. Index. 284pp. 9 × 12.
23766-4 Pa. $9.95

OBELISTS FLY HIGH, C. Daly King. Masterpiece of American detective fiction, long out of print, involves murder on a 1935 transcontinental flight—"a very thrilling story"—NY Times. Unabridged and unaltered republication of the edition published by William Collins Sons & Co. Ltd., London, 1935. 288pp. 5⅜ × 8½. (Available in U.S. only)   25036-9 Pa. $4.95

VICTORIAN AND EDWARDIAN FASHION: A Photographic Survey, Alison Gernsheim. First fashion history completely illustrated by contemporary photographs. Full text plus 235 photos, 1840-1914, in which many celebrities appear. 240pp. 6½ × 9¼.   24205-6 Pa. $6.00

THE ART OF THE FRENCH ILLUSTRATED BOOK, 1700-1914, Gordon N. Ray. Over 630 superb book illustrations by Fragonard, Delacroix, Daumier, Doré, Grandville, Manet, Mucha, Steinlen, Toulouse-Lautrec and many others. Preface. Introduction. 633 halftones. Indices of artists, authors & titles, binders and provenances. Appendices. Bibliography. 608pp. 8⅜ × 11¼.   25086-5 Pa. $24.95

THE WONDERFUL WIZARD OF OZ, L. Frank Baum. Facsimile in full color of America's finest children's classic. 143 illustrations by W. W. Denslow. 267pp. 5⅜ × 8½.   20691-2 Pa. $5.95

FRONTIERS OF MODERN PHYSICS: New Perspectives on Cosmology, Relativity, Black Holes and Extraterrestrial Intelligence, Tony Rothman, et al. For the intelligent layman. Subjects include: cosmological models of the universe; black holes; the neutrino; the search for extraterrestrial intelligence. Introduction. 46 black-and-white illustrations. 192pp. 5⅜ × 8½.   24587-X Pa. $6.95

THE FRIENDLY STARS, Martha Evans Martin & Donald Howard Menzel. Classic text marshalls the stars together in an engaging, non-technical survey, presenting them as sources of beauty in night sky. 23 illustrations. Foreword. 2 star charts. Index. 147pp. 5⅜ × 8½.   21099-5 Pa. $3.50

FADS AND FALLACIES IN THE NAME OF SCIENCE, Martin Gardner. Fair, witty appraisal of cranks, quacks, and quackeries of science and pseudoscience: hollow earth, Velikovsky, orgone energy, Dianetics, flying saucers, Bridey Murphy, food and medical fads, etc. Revised, expanded In the Name of Science. "A very able and even-tempered presentation."—The New Yorker. 363pp. 5⅜ × 8.
20394-8 Pa. $6.50

ANCIENT EGYPT: ITS CULTURE AND HISTORY, J. E Manchip White. From pre-dynastics through Ptolemies: society, history, political structure, religion, daily life, literature, cultural heritage. 48 plates. 217pp. 5⅜ × 8½.   22548-8 Pa. $4.95

SIR HARRY HOTSPUR OF HUMBLETHWAITE, Anthony Trollope. Incisive, unconventional psychological study of a conflict between a wealthy baronet, his idealistic daughter, and their scapegrace cousin. The 1870 novel in its first inexpensive edition in years. 250pp. 5⅜ × 8½. 24953-0 Pa. $5.95

LASERS AND HOLOGRAPHY, Winston E. Kock. Sound introduction to burgeoning field, expanded (1981) for second edition. Wave patterns, coherence, lasers, diffraction, zone plates, properties of holograms, recent advances. 84 illustrations. 160pp. 5⅜ × 8¼. (Except in United Kingdom) 24041-X Pa. $3.50

INTRODUCTION TO ARTIFICIAL INTELLIGENCE: SECOND, ENLARGED EDITION, Philip C. Jackson, Jr. Comprehensive survey of artificial intelligence—the study of how machines (computers) can be made to act intelligently. Includes introductory and advanced material. Extensive notes updating the main text. 132 black-and-white illustrations. 512pp. 5⅜ × 8½. 24864-X Pa. $8.95

HISTORY OF INDIAN AND INDONESIAN ART, Ananda K. Coomaraswamy. Over 400 illustrations illuminate classic study of Indian art from earliest Harappa finds to early 20th century. Provides philosophical, religious and social insights. 304pp. 6⅜ × 9⅜. 25005-9 Pa. $8.95

THE GOLEM, Gustav Meyrink. Most famous supernatural novel in modern European literature, set in Ghetto of Old Prague around 1890. Compelling story of mystical experiences, strange transformations, profound terror. 13 black-and-white illustrations. 224pp. 5⅜ × 8½. (Available in U.S. only) 25025-3 Pa. $5.95

ARMADALE, Wilkie Collins. Third great mystery novel by the author of *The Woman in White* and *The Moonstone*. Original magazine version with 40 illustrations. 597pp. 5⅜ × 8½. 23429-0 Pa. $9.95

PICTORIAL ENCYCLOPEDIA OF HISTORIC ARCHITECTURAL PLANS, DETAILS AND ELEMENTS: With 1,880 Line Drawings of Arches, Domes, Doorways, Facades, Gables, Windows, etc., John Theodore Haneman. Sourcebook of inspiration for architects, designers, others. Bibliography. Captions. 141pp. 9 × 12. 24605-1 Pa. $6.95

BENCHLEY LOST AND FOUND, Robert Benchley. Finest humor from early 30's, about pet peeves, child psychologists, post office and others. Mostly unavailable elsewhere. 73 illustrations by Peter Arno and others. 183pp. 5⅜ × 8½. 22410-4 Pa. $3.95

ERTÉ GRAPHICS, Erté. Collection of striking color graphics: *Seasons, Alphabet, Numerals, Aces* and *Precious Stones*. 50 plates, including 4 on covers. 48pp. 9⅜ × 12¼. 23580-7 Pa. $6.95

THE JOURNAL OF HENRY D. THOREAU, edited by Bradford Torrey, F. H. Allen. Complete reprinting of 14 volumes, 1837–61, over two million words; the sourcebooks for *Walden*, etc. Definitive. All original sketches, plus 75 photographs. 1,804pp. 8½ × 12¼. 20312-3, 20313-1 Cloth., Two-vol. set $80.00

CASTLES: THEIR CONSTRUCTION AND HISTORY, Sidney Toy. Traces castle development from ancient roots. Nearly 200 photographs and drawings illustrate moats, keeps, baileys, many other features. Caernarvon, Dover Castles, Hadrian's Wall, Tower of London, dozens more. 256pp. 5⅜ × 8¼. 24898-4 Pa. $5.95

CATALOG OF DOVER BOOKS

AMERICAN CLIPPER SHIPS: 1833–1858, Octavius T. Howe & Frederick C. Matthews. Fully-illustrated, encyclopedic review of 352 clipper ships from the period of America's greatest maritime supremacy. Introduction. 109 halftones. 5 black-and-white line illustrations. Index. Total of 928pp. 5⅜ × 8½.
25115-2, 25116-0 Pa., Two-vol. set $17.90

TOWARDS A NEW ARCHITECTURE, Le Corbusier. Pioneering manifesto by great architect, near legendary founder of "International School." Technical and aesthetic theories, views on industry, economics, relation of form to function, "mass-production spirit," much more. Profusely illustrated. Unabridged translation of 13th French edition. Introduction by Frederick Etchells. 320pp. 6⅛ × 9¼. (Available in U.S. only)
25023-7 Pa. $8.95

THE BOOK OF KELLS, edited by Blanche Cirker. Inexpensive collection of 32 full-color, full-page plates from the greatest illuminated manuscript of the Middle Ages, painstakingly reproduced from rare facsimile edition. Publisher's Note. Captions. 32pp. 9⅜ × 12¼.
24345-1 Pa. $4.95

BEST SCIENCE FICTION STORIES OF H. G. WELLS, H. G. Wells. Full novel *The Invisible Man,* plus 17 short stories: "The Crystal Egg," "Aepyornis Island," "The Strange Orchid," etc. 303pp. 5⅜ × 8½. (Available in U.S. only)
21531-8 Pa. $4.95

AMERICAN SAILING SHIPS: Their Plans and History, Charles G. Davis. Photos, construction details of schooners, frigates, clippers, other sailcraft of 18th to early 20th centuries—plus entertaining discourse on design, rigging, nautical lore, much more. 137 black-and-white illustrations. 240pp. 6⅛ × 9¼.
24658-2 Pa. $5.95

ENTERTAINING MATHEMATICAL PUZZLES, Martin Gardner. Selection of author's favorite conundrums involving arithmetic, money, speed, etc., with lively commentary. Complete solutions. 112pp. 5⅜ × 8½.
25211-6 Pa. $2.95

THE WILL TO BELIEVE, HUMAN IMMORTALITY, William James. Two books bound together. Effect of irrational on logical, and arguments for human immortality. 402pp. 5⅜ × 8½.
20291-7 Pa. $7.50

THE HAUNTED MONASTERY and THE CHINESE MAZE MURDERS, Robert Van Gulik. 2 full novels by Van Gulik continue adventures of Judge Dee and his companions. An evil Taoist monastery, seemingly supernatural events; overgrown topiary maze that hides strange crimes. Set in 7th-century China. 27 illustrations. 328pp. 5⅜ × 8½.
23502-5 Pa. $5.95

CELEBRATED CASES OF JUDGE DEE (DEE GOONG AN), translated by Robert Van Gulik. Authentic 18th-century Chinese detective novel; Dee and associates solve three interlocked cases. Led to Van Gulik's own stories with same characters. Extensive introduction. 9 illustrations. 237pp. 5⅜ × 8½.
23337-5 Pa. $4.95

Prices subject to change without notice.
Available at your book dealer or write for free catalog to Dept. GI, Dover Publications, Inc., 31 East 2nd St., Mineola, N.Y. 11501. Dover publishes more than 175 books each year on science, elementary and advanced mathematics, biology, music, art, literary history, social sciences and other areas.